I0223913

7 TIPS TO SELF-FULFILMENT IN LIFE

Sunday Adelaja

7 TIPS TO SELF-FULFILMENT IN LIFE
©2017

ISBN 978-966-1592-78-9

Sunday Adelaja
Kyiv, Ukraine
All rights reserved
sundaydelajablog.com

This is the foundation upon which this book is written, No one is better than you, they only converted better. The so-called idols we have, our mentors, celebrities, billionaires, the innovators and inventors of our age are not better than you, they've only converted their time better than you.

Cover Design by Olexandr Bondaruk

7 TIPS TO SELF-FULFILMENT IN LIFE
Golden Pen Limited
Milton Keynes, United Kingdom
All rights reserved
goldenpenpublishing.com

Table of Contents

PREFACE

This book presents you with 7 simple steps that you can follow to attain self-fulfillment. It is a book that will let you know that success is a possibility. Your life and destiny are not in the hands of some mysterious power at the back of your village somewhere. Neither is it in the backyard of your stepmother. More so, your destiny and future do not depend on the economy of your nation nor on the political party that is in power.

There are concrete and specific steps you could take to come to self-fulfillment. These steps are not many, they are only 7. As you go through this 7 simple steps, it is my belief that you will be able to set yourself free from the shackles of all forms of limitations.

As I clock 50 years of age, I have tried and tested these simple steps and they have worked for me and many others. Hence, I have decided to include this as one of the 50 books I have written to commemorate my birthday celebration.

I pray and hope that you will immediately step out to put into practice, these golden steps.

For the Love of God, Church and Nation.

Dr. Sunday Adelaja

INTRODUCTION

"There are certain things that are fundamental to human fulfillment. The essence of these needs is captured in the phrase "to live, to love to learn, to leave a legacy" The need to leave a legacy is our spiritual need to have a sense of meaning, purpose, personal congruence and contribution"

– Steven R Covey.

What are we talking about here? It is self-fulfillment. That seemingly elusive heart desire of all mankind. From morning till night, night till morning, people all over the globe are in search of it. They are in search of the realization of their hopes and ambitions. They are in search of the happiness and satisfaction that comes from fully utilizing their skills and talents to achieve what they have always wanted in life.

As a matter of fact, they are in desperate pursuit of the pleasure and a feeling of completion that comes from realizing their deepest desires and highest capabilities. Hence, man turns to different avenues and takes several routes in order to achieve this fulfillment.

For example, man goes out of his ways to acquire a quality education and thereafter seeks to find a good job.

Even after getting the job, he doesn't stop there as he goes in search of love, wealth, money, beauty, fame, status, power, recognition so that peradventure some or all of these might bring him the fulfillment his heart craves for.

It is only at the end of all these acquisitions that he comes to the realization that physical parameters do not equate to being fulfilled in life.

Isn't the same true for you? Isn't it true that your life-long quest is to have a life of deep meaning and one that satisfies you completely? Isn't that the same reason for which you attended all the schools that you did right from elementary class to high school and even onto college. Is it not for the same reason also that you strive for a successful career?

The truth is that all of humanity longs for that satisfaction of self-fulfillment. We all have individual goals that we want to achieve in our life-time. The combination of all these dreams, desires, goals, ambitions that we have for our lives and their realization through our own efforts is what gives rise to self-fulfillment for us.

"There is no fulfillment in things whatsoever. And I think one of the reasons depression reigns supreme amongst the rich and famous is some of them thought those things will bring them happiness. But what in fact does is having a cause, having a passion. And that is really what gives life its true meaning"

- Ben Carson

No matter where you are in your life today or what your experience has been so far, I can tell you categorically that you have picked up the right book. You have picked up a book that hands out to you on a platter the solution to your endless search for fulfillment in life. And you are just about to discover that fulfillment is not only a possible to a few in life but it is possible to you as well.

In this book, I've detailed seven golden tips to a life of self-fulfillment. I reveal proven strategies that you can apply to your life immediately in order to add true meaning and value to it. Even if you have lived for seventy years without achieving your quest for fulfilment, the information in this book can turn the rest of your life to years spent in fulfillment.

A minister once said that the saddest thing about officiating a funeral is not the death of the body but the death of dreams. He also did say that the wealthiest place on the planet is the cemetery because there you will find endless amounts of potentials never manifested.

It is my conviction that through the application of the principles revealed in this book, such will never be said of you when you are no longer on planet earth. Not only would you have lived a life filled with happiness, satisfaction and fulfillment but your legacy is one that will attest to this truth. This book is the solution to your life-long quest of finding self-fulfillment.

So right along and let's get you started on the path of fulfillment in life.

Sunday Adelaja

PART 1:
Facts About Living A Fulfilled Life

Chapter 1

You Are Greater Than Who You Are Now

Chapter 1
You Are Greater Than Who You Are Now

While growing up as a child in the remote village of Idomila in Nigeria, if anyone had come to me and made the statement that I was greater than who I was, not only would I have laughed at such a person but I probably would have shown that person the sides of my palms as well. Why would I do that, you might wonder? Is it because I'm cruel and unreasonable? Or because I'm uncouth and barbaric? No, far from it.

However, anyone who went through and suffered half of what I suffered as a child might even do worse because he would think the advocate of such a statement was only making fun of him. The honest truth is that there was nothing in my childhood that could have convinced me I was greater than who I was.

So, what happened to me as a child? What would have necessitated such a response from me to someone who is trying to tell me to look beyond myself and realize that "I was greater than who I was back then".

From Nothing TO Greatness

My story is one I have shared in details in my book Olorunwa but just in case you haven't read it yet, I will set the background for the story right here.

As a child, I grew up in the care of my grandmother. My biological mother was a princess who married a man that her family said was socially irresponsible. He was alleged to have abused my mother. So his actions necessitated my mother's family to withdraw her from her matrimonial house while they took her into custody at the family house. This was to prevent my father from harming her and also a way to put an end to the insult he was meting out to her family in general.

Unknown to the council of elders in her family, as at the time she was being taken out of her home, my mum was already pregnant with me for about 6 months. But what had to be done had to be done so my mum kept on living in the family house till it was time for me to be born.

Three years after giving birth to me, my mother remarried and left me in the care of my grandmother. So, I grew up with grandma. The first few years of life passed by without any hassles. Life was filled with happiness and so much peace. Grandma had three other children who were well-educated both home and abroad and had risen to the pinnacle of their careers. They were the bread-winners and sole providers for the family.

From time to time, they visited grandma and I in the village with a lot of goodies.

They even spoke with me about my future asking questions such as "what kind of life would I love to live, which University will I like to attend? What kind of car would I love to drive and whether I preferred studying in Nigeria or overseas? Of course, I was too young to fully grasp the meaning of the questions they were asking me but nevertheless I had a feeling that they were good things so I happily smiled along. One memorable experience from such times was when one of my uncles came back, put me in his car and taught me how to drive even though I was barely 6 years old.

However, my joy was short-lived, the moment death crept into my family and started snatching my family members' away one after the other. The first one to die tragically and in her prime was my aunt who was the only female child to receive a University education and was an important businesswoman in the society.

While the whole family was trying to recover from the shock of her passing away, my uncle who happened to be grandma's last child also died in a most tragic and unexpected manner. He was taking a ride with his fiancée. While traveling along the road, the driver of a trailer that was ahead of him lost control of the vehicle, rolled backwards and crashed into his vehicle, killing him instantly. He was only 29 years old.

As though that wasn't bad enough, the only light left in my family, in terms of my eldest uncle also died under mysterious circumstances few weeks after his younger brother did. He was only but 34 years old and once again was at the peak of his blossoming career. As a matter of fact, the Nigerian government convened a team to inquire into his death, because they were unable to reconcile the fact that the country had lost such a promising young man.

However, the team convened could not come up with anything as the cause of death. The doctors who attended to him only came up with the fact that he was suffering from a mild bout of malaria for which he should have been discharged. Few hours after he was pronounced dead.

This litany of death that plagued my family ended the era of a blissful and tranquil childhood as life took on a dark connotation thereafter. Upon hearing of the death of her third child within 6 months, my grandmother fainted and fell to the ground and couldn't recover her senses for a long period of time. The next one year saw her spending her life in the intensive care unit of a hospital because of the shock she had suffered. And guess who was made to bear the brunt of these devastating situations? Your guess is as good as mine, it was me.

I went from being under the protective and watchful eyes of my grandma to being all by myself at just the age of 6. Can you imagine that? A six year old child, having no one to fend for him but being by himself all alone. That was my situation. Of course, I was put in the care of some relatives presumably, but in reality, I was all by myself.

Grandma survived the trauma and came out of the hospital. Life took on a different turn for me because I had to start following her to the forest to cut and gather wood which we later sold in order to earn a living. Not only this, I also had to hawk corn porridge prepared by grandma early in the morning before going to school. After which I would trek a distance of two and a half kilometers to and fro the neighboring village where the nearest school was.

Note-worthy is the fact that for all these distance I trekked to and fro school, I did it bare-footed. Grandma couldn't afford to get me a footwear for the next six years of my life. Of course by the time I got to school in the mornings I would be too tired to learn and in the afternoons after scouring for woods in the forest, I was also too tired to read my books, do my assignments or revise anything we studied in class that day.

Little wonder, I was a dullard all of those years. I could neither learn anything, retain information, assimilate nor grasp even the most elementary things being taught in class. All those years, I wondered why I was so dull and my mind was so blocked.

Now, imagine, how such a person under that situation could ever reconcile the fact that he was greater than he was. You will agree with me that, that must have be an uphill task.

Not to forget the fact that the sad occurrences that happened to me coupled with the fact that I had to work so hard every day to make a living had turned me into a twisted child. I was broken inwards and didn't fail to unleash my anger on my loving grandmother or anyone else in my way for that matter. Moments of anger saw me going into a fight and destroying grandma's most valuable possessions.

There was a time I dumped her best dresses in a heap of refuse for scolding me. On another occasion, I took some kerosene and doused the walls of her room with it ready to burn down the whole house because she had punished me for something I did. On yet another occasion, I packed together all of her jewelries and buried them at a spot which no one has been able to discover up till date.

All these I did because I had buried so much bitterness and hate in me. You see grandma was the most important personality in my life. She was the dearest of all to my soul but this I didn't even realize until after her death. The cold hands of death snatched her away from me when I was barely 16 years of age. At that time, I was ready to die because I felt that with her death, my end had come also.

How was I going to survive all by myself? Why should grandma be taken away from me in such a brutal manner? Who will love me, care for me and look after me? Why should I go on living when the only person I knew and the only life I had, had been cruelly taken away from me? These and more were some of the questions that ran through my mind as the news of her death slowly sank through me. The last time I had seen her was at the hospital where she was taken to after she was diagnosed with cancer.

It took her death to slap me back into reality and made me decide to forge a path of success for myself in life. The first thing I did was that I learnt her trade of how to prepare pap with her special recipe after which I would put it in small packages and go to sell to the wealthier villagers. And I also continued to go to the forest to gather firewood which I later sold. But the most remarkable of all was when as a 16 year old teenager, I approached the king of my community and requested for a plot of land to plant cassava on but I was magnanimously gifted 7 acres to plant on. That marked a turn-around in my life as the villagers who had earlier written me off as a hopeless case began to see me as a reference point for success.

Why did I take you down this route? It is so that you can know that it doesn't matter how bad your situation may be today, it doesn't even matter how good it is, the truth is that you are greater than who you are right now.

If I who sprang from the obscure and remote village of Idomila in the South-western part of Nigeria. Attended only local community schools. Exposed to all the hardships, sorrows and loss I just described above. Grew up with an illiterate grandmother who didn't understand the value of education. I became a hopeless case whom villagers didn't see anything good in. Couldn't even understand the value of education. I became a hopeless case whom villagers didn't see anything good in. Couldn't even understand the alphabets of my native dialects until I was 10 years of age and never spoke a word in the English language until I was 19 years of age.

There Is A Seed Of Greatness In You

If I who was broken, twisted and bitter with life can rise out of the ashes of my gloomy past to become the pastor of the largest church in Europe today with 99% of them being predominantly white. If I can become the world renowned national transformation expert the world know me to be today. If I can become an author with over 300 books and still counting. If I can become a strategic advisor to several heads of states across different countries of the earth then you can become anything you desire to be and anything you dream of becoming. The key to making all of these happening is all inside you. It is all wrapped up in the statement that you are greater than who you are now.

All the while I was wasting away and languishing in my village, all that I ever needed to become who I have become today was inside of me. I mean the seed of greatness was right in me, trapped up within me, waiting and itching to be discovered, exploited, excavated and brought out into the open. But I couldn't see it, I didn't see it. I didn't know because no one told me and even if someone had told me, I wouldn't have believed and the reason is because I was looking naturally.

I was blinded by the things that were happening to me in the natural. In fact, it got so bad, I wanted to die after grandma drew her last breath. I didn't think there was anything to live for today. I didn't think I was valuable or possessed anything of value that I could add to the world. But several years after, I now see and understand that there are lots and lots of people and reasons to live for. I see that I am relevant to the scheme and operation of things in this world. I see that I've got something of extreme value to add to my world and so do you dear reader.

One of the things I made up my mind to do after grandma died was to make sure I touch the life of everybody I come in contact with positively. I made a resolution to make an impact no matter how big or small in the lives of those I meet. I also made up my mind that I would always do what I had do to help people in record time/right away knowing fully well that there might not be a second chance as was the case with grandma. I didn't have the opportunity to appreciate her or express my gratitude to her until after her death and it hurts my soul till this very day.

So, for you my dear friend, regardless of what you have been told. Regardless of what you have been forced to believe because of the unpleasant circumstances of your life. Regardless of what you have suffered and are still suffering in life today, believe that you are greater than who you are.

Your greatness is not about the things you can see with your optical eyes. It is not about the material acquisitions you possess. The amount of money in your bank account does not determine the size of your greatness inside. Your greatness is a measure of the content of your soul. The content of your inner man. What you possess in your spirit, your values, your beliefs, abilities, potentials, gifts, talents these are the things that make up for your greatness.

To help you get a fuller understanding of the picture I'm trying to paint about your life. Picture an orange fruit. Imagine how small the seed of that orange it. I mean it's so small that you can hold multiples of it in the palm of your hands without anyone one knowing. But how interesting is it to imagine that that small seed is the one that reproduced that round golden orange fruit that you deliciously suck away on. And not to be mistaken, the seed of that orange cannot only produce just one orange fruit but it has the potentials and the capabilities to produce multiple oranges. In fact, just one seed can reproduce an orchard filled with orange.

Oh what I need you to know is that right where you are today, what you need for your next level and to be greater than what you see of yourself in the natural today is all inside of you. Never despise yourself or look down on you. Never feel as though your coming into this world is an accident or a chance happening. As a matter of fact your coming into this world is not a mistake at all. It was designed and orchestrated by God to be so. It is not an accident any way you want to look at it and here is something to prove this to you.

You Were Born A Champion Already

Do you know that it is a scientific fact that each time a man ejaculates, he produces between 2-5millimetres of semen. For better understanding that is about a teaspoon full of semen. And for each ml that is released there are about a 100million sperms. So, roughly an average make adults ejaculates between 200-600 million of sperm each time. What is mind blowing about this though, is the fact that it is only one sperm cell out of these several millions that successfully gets the opportunity to fertilize a woman's egg.

The reason is that in the process of trying to reach the fallopian tube of the woman where the matured egg is present, the sperm cell has to travel through a complex maze of mechanism in the woman's body. Along the way, many of the sperm cells die due to the acidic nature of the woman's vagina. And for the sperm cells that do not die, some of them end up travelling in different direction in the woman's body. In fact, some travel to the empty fallopian tube and eventually die there but this isn't all. Of the several hundreds' that eventually arrive at the tube that contains the ripe egg, only one of them succeeds in fertilizing the egg and all the other ones die off.

Now, think on this amazing concept. Who knows how many sperm cells were released during your conception. 200 million, 300million or 600 million? Who knows how many of these millions started the race to get to where your mom's egg was waiting ready to be fertilized. And who knows how many eventually made it to the right tube, surrounded your mom's egg and fought for a chance to be the one to penetrate it and bring about your conception.

But guess what? You are the only one who made it of all the several millions of cells. You are the champion who defeated so many others to make it to this world. In spite of all the hurdles, barriers, challenges you had to go through to fertilize your mom's egg, you didn't give up, you made it through. You fought and conquered and made a grand entrance into this world. That makes you a fighter, a winner and a champion, a man who does not give up no matter the odds against him. Regardless of what the circumstances of your life have tried to make you believe, you are a hero who deserves his own applause.

My friend, you are not an accident of mistake. You didn't just appear by chance on this earth. Your birth in this world was orchestrated, signed and sealed by God and there is a purpose for your being on earth. There is something you have within you that only you can contribute to this world. There is an assignment only you can fulfill in this world. There is a vacuum, a void that only you can fill in this world. That is the reason why you made it to the world in the first instance. Do not lose hope. Do not be discouraged either and don't be downcast. You are bigger who you are today. You are greater than what you can see about yourself today. There is something more to you than meets the eye.

Chapter 2

What is Your Intuition Telling You?

Chapter 2
What Is Your Intuition Telling You?

Now that we have gotten the fact that you are greater than who you are out of the way, let us explore another truth. I know that for most people because of the many trials and challenges you have had to go through in life, they may not be quick to accept the fact that they are greater than who they are today. Yet, one thing I know for sure is that somewhere deep inside you there, you actually feel like and believe that you are greater than who you are now. Somewhere deep down inside you, there is this conviction that there is more to your life than what it seems to be now. And yes, you are absolutely right!

The proof is this, in spite of all the hardship, shame, disappointments, difficulties, failures and setbacks that you have had to endure as a person, why didn't you give up? Why didn't you just throw in the towel? Why didn't you swallow poison, cut yourself with a knife, jump down a bridge and end your life?

Whydidyoukeeptellingyourself"I'lltryonemoretime" I'll consider this new opportunity or I'll give this business/career another shot? Why do you keep telling yourself,

I will find another way to make it work; whatever it is? Why do you tell yourself if only I can improve myself, get an advanced education, I will have a better chance? You know the simple answer? It is because you intuitively sense that there's more to you than you're seeing right now. It's because you believe that you're greater than who you are now.

In fact, that is why you still allow yourself to dream of a better day, a better future, a better tomorrow? That is also the reason why there you might still have a discontent or dissatisfaction in your soul even when you have accomplished great heights for which other people are looking up to you as a source of inspiration? And that is the reason why you allowed yourself to pick this book "7 Tips To Self-Fulfillment" to read.

It's because you believe in your greatness. You know within yourself that you are greater than who you are now. You are assured in the knowledge that this is not all there is to you. You intuitively sense that you are greater than who you are now and you know what? You are right. I mean you are right to believe that you are greater than who you see yourself to be today. Actually this subconscious belief you have about your greatness is a powerful one that should transcend from your subconscious into your conscious mind.

Let's take a trip down memory lane to your childhood. When you were young and a child, what did you dream about? Who did you see yourself becoming in life?

What kind of future did you envisage for yourself? What are the things you wanted to achieve and accomplish as a person? Isn't it true that you wanted to live a good, rich, successful and prosperous life? Isn't it true that you dreamt of owning all the beautiful and nice things of life? The cars, the jets, beautiful homes, a thriving career, a happy family and all of that. Of course you did.

Even for those who grew up in abject poverty, in their minds they dissociated themselves from that poverty and had their sights on something better for their future. That is the power of intuition. It is what made you know that you deserve better and you are actually made for better even when there was nothing in the natural to justify this belief. You just knew somewhere deep within your soul that you were made for greatness.

What is Intuition?

According to Cambridge dictionary – *Intuition is an ability to understand or know something immediately based on your feelings rather than fact.*

Intuition is knowing something without being able to explain how you came to that conclusion rationally. It is that mysterious "gut feeling" or "instinct" that often turns out to be right in retrospect.

Sophy Burnham, bestselling author of the Art of Intuition describes intuition as being different from thinking. It's different from logic or analysis she says. "It is a knowing without knowing."

There are several synonyms with which the word intuition can be described. Sometimes it's described as gut feeling, innate wisdom, inner sense, instinct, inner voice, spiritual guides as well as the word sixth sense.

The word sixth sense is one of the synonyms that are frequently used in the place of intuition. For instance you might have witnessed a scenario where someone took a precaution that was obviously not necessary or it might have even happened to you yourself.

Take for instance, you were going out with a friend with the temperature being as hot as -37c. Logically such a weather is so hot and no one should be expecting it to rain except the weather forecast says so. But, let's assume that as you were going out, your friend slipped an umbrella into her bag. Before you could ask her why she did that, she hinted you on the fact that it was going to rain later that day and so to avoid getting wet, she took the umbrella along with her.

Just to be sure, you went ahead asking her whether she had already checked the forecast for that day but she quipped back that she hadn't. And then you asked her that, if she didn't check the forecast for the day, why is she then so confident that it was going to rain, and she replied you "my sixth sense".What your friend is trying to say basically is that she has no proof that it was going to rain, she cannot even explain it logically yet she is so convinced of the certainty of it through some inner instinct that she left the house with an umbrella.

Hence the word sixth sense comes into play when in spite of the fact that you cannot see a thing, you can't touch it, you can't perceive it with your nostrils, you can't taste it, you can't even hear it yet you believe in its certainty. In other words there is an extra sense "the sixth sense" that makes you believe in the certainty of something that your five senses didn't not pick up.

The good news is that all of us humans possess this extra sense. It is the reason why you may meet somebody for the first time but instinctively you just don't like the person even when he has done you no wrong. It is also the same reason why everyone may be urging you to go in a certain direction but yet you choose to go the opposite and it later turns how that your decision was the right one.

In fact intuitions have helped several people make life-changing decisions in an instant. Some people have attested to the fact that when they were out checking properties and having a hard time deciding on which to buy, the moment they stepped into a particular house, voila, they just knew that was the one and it turned out to be so for them at the end of the day. Many have said the moment they set their eyes on their would be spouse/partner, they just knew she was the one.

Funny enough, intuition or sixth sense or inner instincts isn't limited to humans alone. Even animals do possess it as well. As a matter of fact, time and time again many people have observed that at the exact moment a person who owns a dog dies, the dog starts howling. How did the dog get to know that its master was dead; intuitions.

Your intuitions are not to be taken lightly. They are placed in you to be some sort of guidance for your life. Throughout history and through diverse cultures, our intuitions communicate to us repeatedly in ways that science isn't able to explain just yet. As a matter of fact intuition is so powerful that it has been credited to help troops make quicker judgment during combat that ended up saving lives and for which reason the US military is now investigating its powers.

Also, Ivy Estabrooke, a program manager at the office of the Naval research told the New York Times in 2012 that"

"There is a body of anecdotal evidence, combined with solid research efforts that suggests that intuition is a critical aspect of how, we humans interact with our environment and how, ultimately we make many of our decisions"
"Intuition is seeing with the soul"

– Dean Koontz

"All great men are gifted with intuition. They know without reasoning or analysis what they need to know"

– Alexis Carrel.

"Don't try to comprehend with your mind. Your minds are very limited. Use your intuitions" – Madelaine L'Engel, wrote in A Wrinkle In Time.

Many other great and famous people have attested to the amazing benefits of using their intuitions. One of such people is Oprah Winfrey. In her words she said:

"I've trusted the still small voice of intuition my entire life And the only time I've made mistakes is when I didn't listen. For all the major moves in my life to – Baltimore, to Chicago, to own my own show and to end it – I have trusted my instincts. I take in all the information I can gather. I listen to proposals, ideas and advices. Then I go with my gut feeling, what my heart feels most strongly. I believe it is how God speaks to us"

- Oprah Winfrey

How amazing! Another famous personality who attested to the great powers of intuition is Steve Jobs. In his words he said that:

"Intuition is more powerful than intellect" Steve Jobs
"I rely far more on gut instinct than researching huge amounts of statistics"

Sir Richard Branson

Albert Einstein calls intuition "a sacred gift and also says it is our most valuable asset and one of our most unused senses"
Donald Trump also admits that he built a multi-billion dollar empire by using his intuition.

What all these are telling you is that your intuition is a valuable tool in your life that you mustn't take lightly. When it tells you that you are greater than who you are even when nothing in your life points to that fact, you better believe and start exploring ways to amplify your greatness.

As powerful as your intuitions are, they can either lead you in the right direction or lead you in the wrong one. When your intuitions are properly developed, they lead you in the right direction. When you leave them undeveloped and allow all the thoughts of your heart to cram them, they may lead you in the wrong directions and cause you to make decisions that are fatal and irreversible just as in the case of a Russian pilot I heard of.

In the summer of July 2002, a Russian airliner's computer - guidance system instructed its pilot to ascend as another jet approached in the sky over Switzerland. And at the same time, a Swiss air traffic controller whose computerized system was down offered a human judgment and asked the pilot to descend. Faced with conflicting advice, the pilot's intuitive response was to trust another human's intuition. Tragically, the two planes collided midair, killing everyone onboard.

If the pilot had developed a keen intuitive sense, this need not have been the case. Reason being that our intuitions are not necessarily supposed to be put to use when everything is cool, nice and controllable alone but they should come to play especially in situations when we need to make split seconds decisions and every second counts.

How can you develop your intuition to make it a more effective guide

By Being Mindful And Staying In The Present: Essentially, this means that you should always make effort to stay in the present. Instead of allowing your mind to roam about and dwell on the negative things that have happened to you or even agitating on the nice things you are anticipating, learn to stay in the present. This will help to clear your mind of all clutters and will help you to be able to be able to pick up on the small voice of your intuition.

Employ Your Subconscious When You Go To Bed At Night: To do this what you need to do is to focus on all the questions you couldn't come up with answers to during the day. Now as you lay on your bed and go to sleep, think about all these questions again. Explore various scenarios and possibilities in your mind. As you do, you will be triggering your imagination and putting your subconscious mind to work to supply you with creative answers while you sleep. And for this reason, it is important that you have a pen and paper or any writing material beside you as you go to sleep so you can pen down the answers you come up with when you wake at night.

Employ The Art Of Meditation: Of course there are a thousand and one meditation practices that different people advocate for different things. The one we are talking about here though is the simple act of quieting your mind for few minutes per day. That is, you force yourself into a state where you do not think, analyze or try to rationalize anything but instead you are open to listening to what your inner guide/gut feeling is telling you. Ideas and solution may come to you at all times.

Benefits Of Listening To Your Intuition

Right away, I will just like to highlight a few benefits of listening to your intuitions

• It helps you make better and more integrative decisions.

• It unleashes your creativity and imagination.

• Being in touch with your intuitions helps you prevent the buildup of negative emotions.

• It puts you in touch with your subconscious and helps you uncover hidden truths about yourself and situations in your life.

• It helps you reduce stress by identifying and dealing with problems more effectively.

• It also integrates left brain and right brain functioning hence you have a more complete perspective on issues.

• And finally, perhaps the most important benefit of following your intuition is that it alerts you to the path, people and circumstances that you as a person will find ultimately fulfilling.

How You Can Follow Your Intuition

By stilling your mind. From time to time, you have to learn to quieten your mind. You've got to refuse your mind from wandering in every direction. You've got to bring stillness and quietness into your mind even if your entire life feels chaotic at the moment. Just try to step away from the whole situation. Take a walk in the park. Drive through a quiet part of your city. Go outdoors to a children's playground jut anywhere you can remove your thoughts away from the pressure of your life and just allow your mind to relax, rest and give your intuitive voice the opportunity to communicate with you.

Another way you can follow your intuition is by journaling – When you are having a hard time making a choice or decision. One more time still your mind as much as you can thereafter get out a pen and paper because it's time to write. Let thoughts, ideas flow from you, just keep writing. Somewhere in between those words you pen down, you will find some answers and guidance for your situation. Make sure you are in a place that is quiet, calm and reflective to get the most out of your intuitions. Writing or journaling helps your subconscious mind to open up. The words you put down may not make sense to you at that point in time but eventually they will.

Learn to trust your hunches and gut feelings- If something doesn't feel right, it probably isn't right so don't push it. . Many people have been saved from getting into accidents this way. Some get to the airport and change their flight tickets, others refuse to even venture out of the house for the day not knowing why but they just didn't anyway. Looking back in retrospect, they then appreciate the decision they made.

This does not mean you should become a freak and freak out on everything. The bottom line is to develop your intuition like you would develop any new skills set you are taking on. It is like working out your muscles. The more you do, the stronger it gets over time. When you do this, then learn to trust it.

Also, to follow your intuitions, you've got to turn off your inner critic. By that I mean that voice that wants to explain away everything your soul is trying to tell you. The voice that wants rationality and logicality for your actions. Intuition isn't logical or rational and can't be explained away anyway, so shut the critical voice and trust your gut feelings instead.

Chapter 3

You Have Not Done What You Came To This World For

Chapter 3
You Have Not Done What You Came To This World For

Most of us intuitively sense that we are actually greater than who we are right now. Maybe even you sometimes feel that you have not really done what you came to this world for yet. Well, if truth be told, you are absolutely correct! This best describes the story of Michael Hyatt.

Michael is a popular best-selling author, blogger and speaker. He was named by Forbes as one of the top ten online marketing experts to follow as well as one of the top 50 social media influencers worldwide. His blog, MichelHyatt.com is ranked by google in the top one-half percent of all blogs with millions of page views in a month. But, what is his story? How did he become all of these?

Michael did not start out his life working as a blogger. As a matter, for most of his life, he had always been in the publishing space (field). Through sheer determination and hard work, he quickly rose through the ranks and later on became the Chairman & CEO of Thomas Nelson Publishers; the world's largest publisher of bibles and bible related materials. This was the peak of his career and ordinarily one would have thought that Michael should be satisfied with how far he had come in life.

I mean he was the Chairman cum CEO of publishing firm. Some of the biggest names in the contemporary Christian world patronized his publishing firm to get their works published. The likes of Billy Graham, Max Lucado, Barbara Johnson a large and even Dr. Robert Schuller to mention just but a few.

By every standard and definition of the word, Michel Hyatt was a successful man as he was well known, influential and well respected. But then, Michael was soon to resign and give up his position at Thomas Nelson to pick up a different assignment in life. The fact that he resigned from his enviable job was not the earth-shaking news, it was what he resigned his job to pursue that called for attention.

Michael left Thomas Nelson to become a blogger! A venture that many found demeaning and beneath him. As at the time, he started blogging, it hadn't gained the kind of recognition it has gained today as bloggers were mainly known as people who were struggling though life. Bloggers were considered as people who had nothing much to do with their lives. But according to Michael, that was what he wanted to do.

Even though he had been a publishing heavy weight for years, yet he didn't find fulfilment in that. Somehow, deep within him, he knew that the major thing he wanted to do with his life was writing and not just publishing other people's work. Sharing his knowledge with people through writing and that was exactly what he embarked on. He turned to writing online articles and books all in a bid to share his knowledge.

Note-worthy is the fact that it wasn't all smooth and rosy at the beginning as he had those days when he would publish an article and no one would respond to it. However, Michael kept at it because he found a fulfillment he didn't derive else-where. He understood that this was his calling as well as his passion and years later, his efforts paid off.

As at the time, he put aside his publishing career, he was already 55 years of age, an age when he should have been thinking of retiring and spend the rest of his life soaking up in the sun or playing golf. A time when he should have been chilling and cooling off haven made enough money for himself but this was not to so. He plunged himself headlong into sharing his knowledge with people through his site which has gone ahead to become one of the world's most visited site monthly and one which is ranked as a multi-million dollar one.

"Everyone has inside of him a piece of good news. The good news is that you don't know how great you can be! How much you can love! What you can accomplish! And what your potential is!"

- Anne Frank

So, dear friend, can you beat your chest and say that you have done what you really came to this world to do? Or is there a tiny voice that keeps echoing in your head that you are greater than who you are today and that no matter what your achievements are, you are meant for greater things? If so, that is a voice that has come to guide you to the paths of greatness and fulfillment. Do not ignore it.

Just like Michael, you also might have risen to the pinnacle of success. You might have achieved what your mates and peers have not achieved. You might have even made tremendous amount of money that have earned you the respect of all and sundry. However, all of these put together without pursuing and going after what you were born to do in this world will only spell one thing for you; lack of fulfillment in life.

Stop Chasing Shadows

Man was not created to pursue money, wealth or fame. These are supposed to be the by-products of doing what you came to this world for. So, re-orientate your mind and start pursuing substance instead of shadow. Start going after that which you came into this world for rather than chasing after money, wealth and fame.

There are so many people who have achieved the trio described above in this world but yet they are not fulfilled not satisfied. There is still something missing in their lives. When they were chasing money and the rest, they thought it was going to bring them happiness and fulfillment. And sure enough, it did but for a short period of time. It was later on they realized that these things in themselves do not guarantee true happiness and fulfillment. Don't fall into this mistake. Place fulfilling your mission on earth ahead of pursuing wealth and fame.

"What is money? A man is a success if he gets up in the morning and goes to bed at night and in between does what he wants to do"

– Bob Dylan.

No matter what you have already achieved, you know inside that you are meant for something more. Go in search of that something more and make sure you fulfill it.

Your life's purpose may not look fancy or sophisticated by society's standard. However, once you realize that it is your assignment on earth, go for it with all your might. It is in going after what you were born for that your soul will find rest and fulfillment.

On the flip side of this argument are those who although know that they have not done what they came to this world to do, yet they are so cumbered with the pressure of living from day to day that they are not able to bring themselves to follow after their passion and calling.

All over the world, people take on different jobs and responsibilities in other careers just to keep body and soul together. By body and soul, I mean payment of rent, bills, mortgages and what have you. But in reality this should not be so because your assignment/purpose on earth is not to keep body and soul together. There is a definite reason for your existence in this world. God who created you created you for a purpose and it is your responsibility to find that purpose. Except you find that purpose, your soul will only be a wanderer on earth. You will be engulfed in deep dissatisfaction and unfulfillment.

God is not a careless or mindless being. He doesn't just do things for the sake of doing them. He didn't bring you to this world to add to the statistics of human beings that are already on earth. He rather has a definite assignment for you to carry out. That assignment is your purpose on earth. It is the reason for your being and it is something you must go after.

Truth be told, it may be okay for the time being to take up any job in order to be able to pay your bills. However, while you are at that job, let it keep ringing and echoing in your mind that you are on earth for a unique and definite reason and make up your mind that you will find that reason as soon as possible.

Just for the records, this does not also mean that you should do a wishy-washy job where you are currently working. It rather means that you should do the job to the best of your ability while at the same time doing a soul-search to discover the reason why you are on earth. When you discover it, start pursuing this reason with all your being.

Of course, I know that it's not just as simple as ABC to find the reason why you came to this world let alone have the courage to pursue it. Just relax, we will deal with this in a later chapter of this book but for now let's examine 2 of the major reasons people find it difficult to leave jobs in order to pursue their calling.

Two reasons why people are not able to leave their jobs to fulfill their callings/purpose that will lead them to fulfillment.

1. Lack of adequate finances.
2. Lack of time.

Lack Of Adequate Finances – From what I have come to observe over the years, this is one of the major reasons people aren't able to leave jobs in order to go pursue their callings. They just don't have the finances to take such a bold decision. So, they would rather stay at a job that offers them some sort of security in the form of a paycheck at the end of the month. If this happens to be you, then it might be time to critically evaluate your finances and re-organize it. It must mean that for all the years you have been working, you have been doing so for "Uncle Sam" and not for yourself.

In a bid to avoid getting you flustered, I will quickly define the terminology "Uncle Sam" to you. Uncle Sam is a financial system in the world whereby a man is working and slaving away only to make enough money to pay his bills and nothing more. This kind of practice makes you a slave because you keep on working for money whereas money is supposed to be working for you. The unpalatable side-effect of this is that whatever money you are earning is not useful in helping to secure your financial future. You are not able to carry out investments that will make you financially free and thus you have to be dependent on working at a job all your life.

Living like this makes you trapped in life. Think of it for a moment, even when you discover your calling, you won't be able to just hop and go because questions will stab you from every angle. Questions like: how do I pay my bills? How do I pay my rent? How do I pay my children's fees? How do I pay off my mortgage? How do I pay off my student loan and even much more? You see why I said that you literally become a slave. You become a slave to money and a slave to the "Uncle Sam" system of this world and this will literally make it impossible to attain fulfillment in life.

Don't be deceived my friend, fulfillment cannot be gotten from the place of doing jobs. It can only be found in your place of assignment. So the first thing you want to do is to liberate yourself from the Uncle Sam's system of this world. You've got to find out and discover the rules of money. You have to apply the rules of money that liberates a man financially, makes him super wealthy, give him the freedom to pursue your life's purpose and ultimately leads him to fulfillment in life. By the way I have a whole set of teaching on this in my book "Money Won't Make You Rich"

Lack Of Time: Another common reason people give for not being able to go fulfill their calling is the lack of time. They complain "oh my job takes all my time and I cannot find any extra time to squeeze into fulfill my purpose. Or they say, my schedule is so booked and I just don't have the time for anything else and so on and so forth. From what I have come to observe though, I beg to differ on this subject. I do not believe for once that lack of time is the problem of such people but rather the mismanagement of the available time that they have. Let's look at it together. In most work establishments, people are expected to resume work at 9am in the morning and close from work at 5pm in the evening. That's just 8 hours of the 24 hours in a day.

Yes, you literally spend the greater half of your day in an office or wherever your working place is. But then, what about when you close from work and return to your house in the evenings? What do you spend the rest of your hours doing. A Chinese author has rightly spoken that what you do with your time between the hours of 6pm and 12 midnight every day is what determines your future. I couldn't agree more with that especially if you are working at a job that requires you to be present there from morning till evening. It means you have the rest of the evening to yourself to make a great future happen for yourself.

Many people who used to work at jobs have actually followed this principle and have gone ahead to create their dream life and future. They work at their place of job during the day and use the evenings to pursue their true calling and passion. By so doing, they are enjoying the fulfillment of doing what they were born to do.

You might want to turn to yourself and ask yourself some salient questions right now. Especially if you are one of those people who complain that they don't have enough time away from their work to pursue their calling and fulfill their purpose.

• What do you do between the hours of 6pm and 12 midnight daily?

• Are you busy scrolling through your friend's pictures on Instagram?

• Are you busy chatting up an old school mate on Face book?

• Are you busy whiling away the time gisting, chatting and catching fun or even making needless telephone conversations?

• Or perhaps watching movies and playing games.

It has been established that the average adult spends 14 hours a week just watching television. That's a lot of time just going down the drain and I think you will agree with that. Dear friend, for you to come to fulfillment in life, you must make yourself a slave of your calling, a slave of your purpose and nothing else.

"Let yourself be drawn by the stronger pull of that which you truly love"

\- Rumi

Let your calling, purpose and passion become the pull of your life. Let them be the driving force of your life and you will be amazed at how fulfilling they can really make life for you.

This is not to say that if you have a family, you shouldn't spend time with them. Of course, you should spend good and quality time for that matter. Even if you don't have a family you might need to make some important calls, make some necessary visits, reach out & expand your network and circle of contacts, read up books for your self-development or even go to the gym and carry out some fitness regimen. However, you should also still slot in a couple of hours in the evening every day to carry out your life's purpose and pursue your life's passion. This will inevitably lead you to the path of fulfillment in life.

"Don't compromise yourself. You're all you've got."

-Janis Joplin

Chapter 4

Forget About Your Best

Chapter 4
Forget About Your Best

Have you ever accomplished something really significant in your life before? Have you gotten to that point where you can beat your chest and say that you have done something of worth with your life? That was where Mark Albion was at a certain stage in his life.

Mark Albion is a typical example of a man who had it all. He earned 3 degrees at Harvard University: a bachelor's in economics, an MBA, and a PHD in business economics. In 1982, at the age of 31, he won an appointment in Harvard business school where he taught marketing. His success there was phenomenal and he was constantly referred to as the wunderkind professor of Harvard business school. Although being a professor at his age, he was much younger than many of his students. Nationally, he was recognized as one of America's top young business professors and was profiled on CBS's 60 minutes. At the age of 35, Mark was making money beyond his wildest imagination. He was being described as a hotshot consultant who was getting richer by the minute. As at 1986, he was charging a consulting fees of $5000 per day from the Blue Chip companies who sought his expertise. These Blue Chips Company flew him regularly to their operating quarters to help them fine-tune their brands.

He was also co-owner of a nutritional supplement company that raked in $60million in its first six months. He was on the short-list with one other candidate to become the nutritional company's next chief executive officer and get even extremely wealthier. He was also being courted by the Reagan administration for a subcabinet post. He had unlimited resources at his disposal and also personal wealth of his own. By every definition of the word, he was a successful hotshot and many of his peers envied him.

In spite of all these success, Mark Albion was a miserable man. Time and time again, he wondered to himself that something didn't feel right about his life. He wondered that something vital was missing from his life. All these made him feel like his life was being sucked out of him on a daily basis. Despite these misgivings, Albion couldn't bring himself to give up the good life in Harvard. He was reveling in the glory his work there offered him.

This continued for a long time. The feeling of deep dissatisfaction and unfulfillment were very familiar with him but he trudged along hoping that things would get better and he would start enjoying his work someday. Instead of such a day coming, he rather received a wake-up call that helped him make the decision to find his calling and pursue it.

It so happened that his mother Leni was suffering from cancer. She had been unwell for a period of time before she broke the news to him. In spite of her failing health, his mother had continued to go to work, dragging herself there daily and lying on the floor next to her desk because she could not sit at all. She was there every day because she loved her work so much and found it fulfilling.

Mark Albion then asked himself the ultimate question "Would I do the same for Harvard University?" The answer was an emphatic no. He couldn't see himself dragging his body to work daily to lie on the floor beside his office desk working endlessly for his students at the University and the reason is because he didn't find the work fulfilling.

There and then, he received the courage to stop pursuing the material rewards that kept him bound working for Harvard University and went in search of his life's purpose and assignment. He went in search of his heartbeat; that one thing he could give undeniable commitment to even if his very life was ebbing away. It took him some years but he eventually found that thing. That is, he began sharing inspirational messages through several means; newsletter, speaking from the stage and through books on subjects that mattered to him deeply to motivate, inspire and encourage others. In his words he said

"I have been an educator for most of my life. But I have always gone by the book-not just my book. I didn't have the courage or the confidence to be myself whoever that was. However, for the first time, in my 45 years on earth, I was able to speak at a United Nations

conference in my own style, with my own voice and from my heart. Doing that at that conference marked the beginning of happiness and fulfillment for me."

It was only after this that he found inner peace and satisfaction in life.

"I have seen business moguls achieve their ultimate goals but still live in frustration, worry, and fear. What's preventing these successful people for being happy? The answer is they have focused only on achievement and not fulfillment. Extraordinary accomplishment does not guarantee extraordinary joy, happiness, love, and a sense of meaning. These two skill sets feed off each other, and make me believe that success without fulfillment is failure"

– Tony Robbins

You might be a Mark Albion in your own class today. You might have gone ahead to achieve the material comforts of this life and yet your soul has not found fulfillment. Probably, you have even been thinking that something is wrong with you because in spite of all you have that makes your peers envious, you are still not satisfied. Well, I want you to know that nothing is wrong with you.

What you have been missing all these while is that self-fulfillment cannot be gotten from anything in the physical world. It is only obtainable when you discover what you were truly born for and you pursue it with all your might. And that is what you should begin doing from right now. Find out who you are, what you were born to accomplish on earth and begin to do them. You will be surprised at how your life will turn to a paradise on earth. Every day for you will cause your heart to be lit up with joy and satisfaction.

"People want riches; they need fulfillment."

-Robert Conklin

"To be what we are, and to become what we are capable of becoming, is the only end of life".

-Robert Louis Stevenson

One of the greatest gifts you can give to yourself is to refuse to be satisfied with where you are. Forget about whatever your best might be right now because there is much more to be revealed through you. Your desire and continuous passion will perpetually open doors of fulfillment to you.

"As long as I have a want, I have a reason for living. Satisfaction is death"

– George Bernard Shaw.

There Is More To Be Accomplished

As sad as it may sound, there are some people who have never given the fact that they are greater than who they are right now a thought. These people are largely in 2 categories. The first are those who don't see anything good about their lives in the present, let alone see a greater than the present for themselves. The second are those who have achieved an enviable measure of success and have now become complacent, thinking they have arrived!

For those who don't see anything good about their lives, this is actually very sad because without pondering on the fact that there is greater than what you can see of yourself in the present, you really can't amount to much in life. This mindset issue prevents you from taking the steps necessary to attain this greatness eventually, prevent you from coming to fulfillment. I have come to discover that most times the underlying factor for most people not considering this truth is because they have a low self-esteem of themselves.

The problem of low self-esteem is one that plagues a wide range of people.

It's been reported by Dr. Joe Rubino (the self-esteem book) that up to 85% of the world's population suffer from low self-esteem. Now, that is an alarming percentage of people!

What Exactly Is Low Self Esteem?

According to a google site, low self-esteem is actually a thinking disorder in which an individual views himself as inadequate, unworthy, unlovable, and/or incompetent. Once formed, this negative view of self permeates every thought, producing faulty assumptions and ongoing self-defeating behavior.»

Also according to UCDHS faculty, Low self-esteem is a debilitating condition that keeps individuals from realizing their full potential.

Why The Astronomical Rate Of Low Self-Esteem Sufferers In The World

In seeking an answer to this question, it's imperative to bear in mind that all of our self-esteem beliefs, either positive or negative are usually formed during childhood years. Specifically, they are formed during the first six years of life. This is made possible as a result of the influence our immediate environment has on us. These influence include the interaction we have with our primary caretakers, our parents & guardians specifically but it's not limited to them.

Other influences that play a crucial role in the formation of our self-esteem beliefs include our teachers, siblings, friends and even the media.

All of these influences sends out messages to us from time to time both positive and negative but for some reason, it's only the negative messages that seem to stick.

For example, a study carried out among some female students reports that 80% of them claimed that their negative body image was linked to the negative remarks made by friends and family. In fact reports have it that young girls are more afraid to become fat than they are of nuclear war, cancer or losing their parents. It's that bad!

However, in examining the case of the students who claimed that their negative body image was linked to the negative remarks they had received from both friends and family, if truth be told, negative remarks cannot be the only comments they've gotten about themselves. At one point or the other, these ladies must have been praised or received a form of compliment from some other people. Somehow, those compliments didn't seem to stick with them except for the negative remarks. Eventually, these negative remarks stuck in their minds and helped them form an opinion about themselves that spells "you are not good enough"

Perhaps the biggest cause of the wide-spread problems of low self-esteem is actually the inactions and actions of parents/guardians to their kids. Again, let's look at it this way. For starters, most parents aren't even aware that their children are forming beliefs and opinions about themselves based on their interactions them. And for most parents who realize this, they usually do not know how to stay on track to behave to their children in such a manner that will only help to foster the development of a solid opinion about himself.

This is due to the fact that these parents are rarely aware of the conflict between what they want and what their children are able to understand and do at various ages of their development. So, the parents end up insisting that the child only do what they want even when the child has not developed the mental capability to understand why he should do it.

Take for example, children from the age of 2 upwards are generally talkers. They love to talk, shout, scream and have fun but parents on the other hand may want some quiet. So they try to get the child to keep quiet yet the child has not developed the mental capability to understand why anyone should stop him from talking.

Another example, an average adult wants the house neat and arranged and in good shape. However, this means little or nothing to a preschooler who only thinks of throwing things around carelessly anywhere in the house yet the parents insists that the house should be kept clean.

Now, it's important to understand that parents getting the child to do what is ethically right is not the problem but the mode of communication. While one parent can be frustrated and take out her anger on the child, another parent can exercise great patience and with utmost gentleness get the child to do what she has to do. The same scenario but different forms of communication.

Over time, it is a given that the child who is constantly been screamed at or abused (verbally, physically, psychologically) will begin to feel that she is not good enough and cannot live up to mummy's expectations let alone other people's expectations. Before you know it, self-doubt and low self-esteem creeps into the child's life. Sadly, this is a mistake the majority of parents the world over make such that right from childhood, a lot of children are already being plagued with low self-esteem!

Asides these two factors listed above as the major cause of low self-esteem, difficult and life-threatening crises such as the loss of a loved one or being involved in a debilitating accident can also contribute to the problem of low self-esteem.

Also, when people set impossibly high standards and expectations for themselves but when they are unable to meet with up with, it results in low self-esteem.

Tell-Tale Signs Of People Suffering From Low Self-Esteem

1. **Insecurity:** People who suffer from low self-esteem are usually insecure and are usually plagued with self-doubt. They often compare themselves with other people and usually fall short in their own estimations.

2. **Pessimism:** They are usually pessimist who only view life from the negative angle.

3. **Unhappiness:** They are mostly unhappy and usually withdrawn.

4. **Socially inept:** People who suffer from low self-esteem are usually socially awkward and have poor people skills.

5. **Angry/hostile:** These set of people are usually prone to hostility and anger even when the situation does not warrant it however because of their troubled state of mind that is how they respond most times.

6. **Unmotivated:** People who suffer from low self-esteem are usually without motivation and as a result, they are not able to get things done in their lives and these leads to a feeling of depression and emptiness.

7. **Depressed:** People who suffer from low self-esteem are usually in a constant state of unexplainable sadness and gloominess. That is most times, they themselves can't explain what is making them sad and it's usually an on-going process in their lives.

8. **Dependent/follower:** Low self-esteem sufferers are never proactive in the sense that they do not have the confidence to take decisions that concern their lives. They leave all decision makings to people around them starting

with their friends, to their spouses or just anyone else for that matter.

9. **Poor self-image:** Low self-esteem sufferers also have a poor self-image. They have a poor opinion about themselves. They see themselves as incapable, unlovable and not good enough and they believe that this is the way every other person sees them.

10. **Non-risk-taker:** People who suffer from low self-esteem are often afraid of taking any form of risks. As such, they will rather stay cocooned within a familiar territory.

11. **Lacks self-confidence:** At times people do mistake their show of confidence as having a healthy sense of esteem but in reality one who has a healthy sense of esteem does not go about trying to convince people of his worth. Rather he knows he is good enough and does not need anyone's approval.

12. **Acts out:** Because of their negative perception about themselves, they feel like that is the way every other person will see them and as result of this, they do everything to try to put on a mask and cover up what they perceive as their short comings. In a bid to do this, they pretend to be who they are not. They put on airs, try to appear cocky and confident and they try to impress other people so that they can respect them.

Other Facts To Know About Low Self-Esteem

Low self-esteem is not limited to the "failures and ne'er-do-wells in life". Shockingly, the reverse is the case as a survey carried out amongst the CEOs of billion dollar companies proves that the uber-successful are usually also plagued with this menace. The survey shows that sometimes some of these successful men and women feel like they are undeserving of their success and perhaps one day everything will just vanish and they will be left high and dry. These thoughts diminishes the satisfaction they should have enjoyed from working so hard to achieve those successes.

Low self-esteem often changes people's behavior in ways that act to confirm that the person isn't able to do things or isn't very good," says Chris Williams, Professor of Psychosocial Psychiatry at the University of Glasgow.

Dangers of low self-esteem

Low self-esteem is the #1 cause of not living your dream life, according to Dr. Joe Rubino who has coached thousands around the world to improve their self-esteem

Low self-esteem can sabotage your career, your relationships and your happiness, according to The

University of Texas Counseling and Mental Health Center. If you never feel good enough, you're more likely to stay in unfulfilling relationships and mediocre jobs. More so, you might create walls that keep you from having meaningful relationships with family and friends.

Other dangers of having a low self-esteem includes substance abuse, high teenage pregnancy, eating disorders, violent behaviors, depression, suicide tendencies, high rate of school drop outs and the list goes on.

How To Boost Your Self-Esteem And Increase Your Chances Of Living A Fulfilled Life

The bottom line is that having a low esteem of yourself will definitely sabotage your dreams of living a fulfilled life so, starting from today bring on your a game in order to eradicate this happiness and fulfillment sucking devil called low self-esteem from your life.

In rounding off this chapter, I would love to reiterate the fact that it is of utmost necessity that you look into yourself often and ask the all-important question; Am I really living a fulfilled life or not? If you answer in the affirmative, keep doing what you are doing that is bringing you the fulfillment. If the answer is in the negative, drop all you are doing and start pursuing the path that that you were born for that will ultimately bring you to fulfillment.

Chapter 5

Don't Retire,
Re-fire!

Chapter 5
Don't Retire, Re-fire!

Among several other factors, it is widely agreed that one of the ways to turn out successful in life is to follow those who are successful. Taking the steps, they took and avoiding the mistakes they made is the fastest way to get where they are with less trouble and less road bumps.

I mean, the best way to begin to take your journey towards self-fulfillment is to look out for those people who have achieved the same. Find out what made them succeed and simply do the same. Then search out those who failed, learn why they ending up failing and stay as far away as possible from those mistakes too. After all, it has been said that in a multitude of counsellors, there is safety!

However, beyond learning from others success and mistakes, a good way to begin to chart your course towards self-fulfillment is to get back to your creator and manufacturer. We all agree that no one knows a product better than the manufacturer and yet, we try so hard to attain success and satisfaction in life without paying any attention to the manufacturer. He must have some advice for us on how to maximize our lives and be the best we were created to be don't you think?

Getting Back To The Drawing Board

When we want to build houses, we go to a building engineer or an architect and express our desires to them. Then these professionals take our desires and thoughts about the house and turn them into a plan. The plan takes into consideration all that we want to building to be and have. Then it also takes into consideration all that the building will carry and contain. Virtually everything about the present and future of the building is factored in before construction finally begins.

So the moment we get to construction phase, we are not just building for building sake. We are building according to a predefined plan that was drawn up to fulfill certain desires that we have earlier expressed. When you see the house having several floors, it is because the original desire that gave birth to the building was for several floors.

Assuming that for some reason, the person who wanted to build the house died mid-way into the project, that doesn't mean that the house should die as well. As long as the resources are avaialbe, anyone can go on to complete that building using the plan that was earlier created. Now, guess what! Just as the case is with building houses, the creation of anything of worth begins with a solid plan by the creator. A plan was already set in place for your fulfillment in life before you were ever conceived. Someone already designed the kind of life you should live and how you should function in other to attain fulfillment in life. But sadly, many never attain self-fulfillment because they never get to find out about the plan.

There is a reason why God in His infinite wisdom has decided to make us in His image and likeness. There is a reason why God has created us to look like Him and to function like Him. We will never really live out our full potentials if we don't realize and discover this. We will never really understand what true fulfillment in life is if we never get to function like we were designed to function.

Imagine for a moment that one day, a fish decided that was tired of staying in the water and needed to take a walk. It wanted to know what it feels like to walk on sand and walk on the grass. Let's also assume that someone mysteriously heard the desire of the fish and granted it its wishes. Not only will that be the end of the life of that fish, every single second it stays outside of water will be horrible. It will struggle and struggle all the way until it eventually dies.

Sometimes, the struggles we face are not necessarily because the world is against our success but because we are functioning in the wrong places with the wrong formula. We are just not functioning as we were created to function.

The basis idea behind our creation in the image and likeness of God is so that we can to an extent function and operate like Him! We all came factory fitted and designed to function like God and not as we wish or desire to function. You were not created to function as the society intends for you to function either. Actually, the discovery of how God functions will be a cool way to begin to position yourself for real fulfillment in life.

Over the course of the rest of this book, we will be looking at some of them but for now, let's take a look at the fact that you were not created to live for retirement!

You Were not Created To Retire

All over the world today, the subject of retirement has taken center stage and I am sorry to say that this is so sad. It is so bad that as soon as people graduate from college, when they should be ready to face life head on, the society begins to prompt them to plan and prepare for retirement. The idea of retirement is already woven into the system the find themselves. So from the first day at work, new graduates are already being programed to plan and prepare for retirement when in the real sense they should just be starting to live.

Some people even pride themselves in being able to retire at the age of 35! While others have made early retirement the sole goal of their lives and time on earth!

"Preparation for old age should begin not later than one's teens. A life which is empty of purpose until 65 will not suddenly become filled on retirement."

\- Dwight L. Moody

Many have even taken the words of D.L Moody above out of context to assume that what he is saying is that they should begin planning for retirement day. Whereas in effect, what he was pointing out here was the importance of living on purpose from day one up until retirement.

Yes, I understand the idea of preparing for old age. I understand the idea of planning for the days when you might not be as strong to run around and carry out labor in the way that you do now. But for crying out loud, were you created to toil and labor just to secure the days of retirement?

Were you really born to work hard in the early days of your life so that the later days can be taken care of? Was it truly in the plan and design of the manufacturer that you should only be active in the early days of your life and then live the rest on a beach somewhere in the Caribbean Island? Shouldn't your life be worth much more than all that?

My dear friend, there is more to living a satisfying and fulfilling life than working all years only to retire to the beaches on the Islands. There is much more to your life than for you to start planning to waste away the later days when you should be busy taking mountains, accomplishing great things and laying down legacies for the next generation.

The problem with this "retirement" mindset is that it rubs you of the true value of work. It deprives you of the opportunity to do the work of your life. In fact, for many people, the need to secure the future determines where they work rather than the fulfillment of their destinies. Then they turn around after 65 to be wondering what they have done with their lives. Well, what you have done is to secure a retirement without ever living ... What a tragedy!

Life doesn't end at retirement my dear. Life isn't designed for you to wind up in a reclining chair at 65. The desire of the manufacturer and giver of life wasn't that you should become useless to yourself and the world simply because you are now 65.

"I actually think the whole concept of retirement is a bit stupid, so yes, I do want to do something else. There is this strange thing that just because chronologically on a Friday night you have reached a certain age... with all that experience, how can it be that on a Monday morning, you are useless?"

- Stuart Rose

I couldn't agree less with Stuart Rose on this. How can you tell someone that just because he finally turned 65 on Friday, come Monday he has become useless or better still too old?

What happens to the wealth of experience he has gathered over the years? What happens to the character he has developed over the years? Haven't you hear them say that life begins at 40?

The fact remains that from the moment you came to the realization that you are a human person, your greatest pursuit in life should be to discover why you are here in the first place. Then from the day you discover why you came, your greatest pursuit should be to fulfill the purpose for which you were sent here period!

Let's Redefine Work

Work isn't meant to be something you get involved with just so you can get paid and live. Work wasn't meant to be something you only do because of the money involved. In fact, if the motivation behind the job you do is money, then you are a confirmed slave of money and that my friend is a shame. No one ever came to self-fulfillment by working for money so do not think you will either.

A few months ago, a mentee couple of mine came to see me in my house. Among other things they came to see me for, they had some questions they wanted to ask me. One of the questions they asked was "how do you manage to prioritize and keep your focus on your assignment in life in the midst of distractions?"

I immediately understood where they were coming from and my answer was a very simple one. I said it was all about becoming a slave to purpose. I explained that by becoming a slave to purpose, I mean submitting yourself to your purpose such that it becomes the governor and determining factor of every move you make in life.

Take for example, if you were a single, then becoming a slave to purpose will influence the kind of person you get married to. If you were looking for a job and had to choose between two or more job offers, being a slave to your purpose will help you decide on the best choice for you as well. It simply means that you only move when the destination in view favors the fulfillment of your purpose and assignment in life.

«The successful warrior is the average man, with laser-like focus.»

- Bruce Lee

If you must live a fulfilling life my dear, then you should never get your eyes off the reason and basis for that fulfillment. According to Bruce Lee, an average person with laser-like focus on his purpose and assignment will actually be more successful than a "superman" without focus on what matters most.

That is why I said if the reason and motivation for going to work is just the money you earn, then you have made yourself a slave of money rather than a slave of your purpose. And guess what! Like I said in my other book – **Money Won't Make You Rich**, money is a bad master but a good slave.

When money is your master, it never leads you to self-fulfillment. When money is all that matters to you, living a fulfilled life will always elude you. The more you try to acquire it, the farther away you will be from living a fulfilling life.

As a matter of fact, that is the reason why several rich people in the world today are still not satisfied with their lives. I can't begin to enumerate the encounters I have had with rich and financially well to do people who still aren't satisfied with life. People who should otherwise be cool with their lives but still feel a void they don't know how to go about filling. By the way, let me tell you upfront that nothing can be more frustrating than having acquired the goods of this world and still not being satisfied.

It's like when a someone has invested his years into getting a university education in hopes that when they get out of school, they will be able to secure a good paying job. But when they come out and are faced with the harsh realities of life, they often end up frustrated and wondering if there was a need to have put in the investment in the first place.

What's The Whole Idea Of Working?

My dear, in other for you to come to experience true fulfillment in life, you have to understand the whole idea of working. You have to get to realize that the whole idea of working is actually for you to get involved in the production of goods and service that improve the lives of other people. Working should be aimed at you getting involved in improving and bettering other people's lives by offering contributing your quota to providing them what they need in their lives. The whole idea of working is to enable you fulfill your personal purpose in life and ultimately become fulfilled.

So rather than start planning for the days of retirement when you have barely even lived, why don't you begin by finding out the meaningful assignment you were born for? Of a certainty, no one who ever truly found out what they were here for prepared to retire. No one who ever really got to discover their unique assignment and went after it considered that at a particular age, they will have to retire. Only people with jobs rather than life assignments retire.

Find out what you are here for and go all out, working tirelessly to accomplish it. Then when it all finished, you check out of the world knowing that you came, you saw and you conquered. You came, you identified your assignment and you endeavored to fulfill it. I will talk a bit more about exactly how you can discover that assignment you were born for in a latter chapter so just read on for now.

Why Advocate For People To Work All Their Lives?

Someone reading this right now might be wondering, "what is the rationale behind advocating that people should work and labor all their lives? Isn't it appropriate that at some stage, a man who has worked since his youth should sit down and rest?"

Well, it's not as much about working all your life as it is about doing meaningful work. It's all about doing something meaningful with your life irrespective of your age.

'Retiring' - within that word is 'tiring,' and I'm not tired. I don't believe in retirement, really."

- Theodore Bikel

Oh how true this is! Why should someone be forced to take the back sit in life simply because of their age? Why should someone who otherwise could have been a resource center of wisdom and experience be sent home because he is 65 already?

Maybe for those who were involved with a job only for the money, retirement would be a great idea. In fact, it would be nice and proper for them to retire as early as possible. That way, they have enough time to pursue the real course of their lives. Otherwise, get that word out of your vocabulary. We work and stay active for as long as we have breath in our nostrils period!

According to Theodore Bikel, within the word "retiring" is the word tiring! That only applies to people who are tired of life or what they are doing. And one thing you can be rest assured of is that no one who ever found his place of assignment ever got tired carrying out that assignment. In fact, the longer they lived, the better they became at carrying out the assignment and the more willing they are to continue doing just that!

Don't let your age lie to you. Don't fall for the deception of the society in which we live in. the idea of retirement is completely against the idea of living a purposeful life. So rather than planning on retiring, think how you can become more relevant in the scheme of things as your age. I call it "triumphant aging".

Author Harry Bernstein and humanitarian Clara McBride Hale are two people who exemplify these themes.

Bernstein was born in Stockport, England in 1910 and began his education as an architect. But when his teacher discouraged his career choice, he decided to pursue a writing career and moved to New York to accomplish his goal. Although he made a living as a writer, his wife, Ruby, had to work as a school secretary to subsidize the family income. He did have one novel published, but it wasn't successful. Undaunted, Bernstein continued to write, penning more than 20 novels that were never published.

In 2007, at age 97, he wrote an autobiographical novel, **The Invisible Wall**, which received critical acclaim. The book poignantly described the "invisible wall" that separated the Jewish and Christian sections of his home town. At age 98, he published, **The Dream**, which told the story of his family's move to America. Because these two books were so successful, he was awarded the Guggenheim Fellowship at age 98 to pursue his writing.

Imagine what he would have missed out on if he had gone with the general notion of retirement at the age of 65! He would have quite from the attainment of his life's mission and true fulfillment, 33 years before he could have attained it.

At 99, he published the third book in the series, **The Golden Willow: The Story of a Lifetime of Love,** about his marriage to Ruby and later years. Today, his novels have been translated into several languages. Bernstein stated:

"If I had not lived until I was 90, I would not have been able to write this book...It could not have been done, even when I was 10 years younger. I wasn't ready. God knows what other potentials lurk in other people, if we could only keep them alive well into their 90s."

- Harry Bernstein

My friend, who knows what potentials you are sitting on and probably suppressing because of the idea of retirement that the society has sold to you. You weren't created to retire but to keep on refiring and making a difference until you draw your last breath.

Another inspiring story in this light is that of Clara McBride Hale. When her husband died, she had to support herself and her three small children. Not wanting to leave her children unsupervised for extended periods of time, she opened a day care in her Harlem neighborhood. Many of the children in her care stayed overnight because their parents worked as domestics. She then decided to become a foster parent and raised 40 foster children, all of whom pursued a college education.

At 64, after 28 years, she retired from the foster care system. Soon after, her daughter referred a drug-addicted mother and baby to Hale for help. Before long, she was caring for all this mother's drug-addicted children – thought she had officially retired from this job!

As the word spread throughout New York City, more and more drug-addicted babies were left in Hale's care. During the first year and a half, her family provided financial and other support to keep her mission going. Then, the Borough of Manhattan president, Percy Sutton, arranged public funding. Also, John Lennon left provisions for support of Hale House in his will.

In 1975, Hale House moved to 122nd Street where it remains today. After successfully reuniting hundreds of families, only 12 children had to be placed for adoption. At age 85, Clara McBride Hale was honored by President Ronald Reagan for her humanitarian work. She later stated:

"I'm not an American hero, I'm just someone who loves children."

\- Clara McBride Hale

"Triumphant aging," as exemplified by Bernstein and Hale, is a counter perspective to the pervasive negative beliefs about aging and retiring. In all honesty, if you haven't found something from which you cannot consider retiring, then you haven't really found a reason to be alive in the first place. You might as well, not be living …

That is why I am glad that you are reading this book right now. You have come to the right place to discover what true fulfillment in life really is and how to attain it in your own life.

Do you, your relatives or friends have untapped potentials or abandoned dreams? Do you have hopes that seem far-fetched and elusive? If so, consider the words of George Elliot who said:

"It's never too late to be what you might have been."

\- George Elliot

Beginning today, you can open up a new chapter in your life. You can turn a new leaf that will guarantee you of a fulfilled life for the rest of your days.

Even The Heroes Of Faith Didn't Retire!

To further illustrate this point of a no-retirement life, I will like you to consider the heroes of faith for a moment. Take a look at the men and women who received good recommendations from God in the course of their lives. How many of them really got to that point in their lives where they thought they had worked enough and it was now time for relaxation? How many of them winded up their lives holidaying on an island somewhere?

Look at Abraham for example, up until his last breath, he was active in pursuing after the fulfillment of the promise and covenant made to him by God. What about Moses? Did he have the luxury of an end of life holiday? I don't think so.

Why then are you planning on one? Why are you looking forward to a work free life when you could be busy changing lives and making the world a better place than you met it?

«Twenty years from now you will be more disappointed by the things that you didn't do than by the ones you did do. So throw off the bowlines. Sail away from the safe harbor. Catch the trade winds in your sails. Explore. Dream.

- Discover.» Mark Twain

Instead of retiring, consider re-firing yourself to do and be all that you were born for.

Interesting Facts About Retirement

As I round up on this idea of retiring and the adverse effect it has on us, I want to point out a few important facts about retirement.

A study found that after giving up work, the average adult was 60 per cent more likely to have at least one diagnosed illness. Retirement was also found to increase the risk of depression by 40 per cent and the chance of being on medication by 60 per cent!

Moreso, retirees were 40 per cent less likely to declare themselves in either 'very good' or 'excellent' health than those still working.

Researchers from the London-based Institute of Economic Affairs think-tank surveyed as many as 9,000 adults aged 50 to 70 from 11 European countries.

Participants filled in detailed questionnaires about their health and wellbeing before retirement and at various stages afterwards. The study tried to account for the fact that some people will retire due to health problems.

But lead researcher Gabriel Sahlgren pointed out that retirement is such a life-changing event that it can actually be far more stressful than continuing to work.

For years now, researchers have been trying to figure out whether the act of retiring, or retirement itself, is good for health, bad for it, or neutral. A new salvo comes from researchers at the Harvard School of Public Health.

They looked at rates of heart attack and stroke among men and women in the ongoing U.S. Health and Retirement Study. Among 5,422 individuals in the study, those who had retired were 40% more likely to have had a heart attack or stroke than those who were still working. The increase was more pronounced during the first year after retirement, and leveled off after that.

The results, reported in the journal Social Science & Medicine, are in line with earlier studies that have shown that retirement is associated with a decline in health. But others have shown that retirement is associated with improvements in health, while some have shown it has little effect on health.

In their paper, Moon and her colleagues described retirement as a "life course transition involving environmental changes that reshape health behaviors, social interactions, and psychosocial stresses" that also brings shifts in identity and preferences. In other words, moving from work to no work comes with a boatload of other changes. "Our results suggest we may need to look at retirement as a process rather than an event," said lead study author J. Robin Moon, who is now a senior health policy advisor to New York Mayor Michael Bloomberg.

These changes may be why retirement is ranked 10th on the list of life's 43 most stressful events. Some people smoothly make the transition into a successful retirement. Others don't.

For four decades, Dr. George E. Vaillant, professor of psychiatry at Harvard Medical School, and numerous colleagues talked with hundreds of men and women taking part in the Study of Adult Development. Initially focused on early development, the study now encompasses issues of aging, like retirement.

When researchers asked study participants 80 and older what made retirements enjoyable, healthy, and rewarding, four key elements emerged:

Forge a new social network. You don't just retire from a job—your retire from daily contact with friends and colleagues. Establishing a new social network is good for both mental and physical health.

Play. Activities such as golf, bridge, ballroom dancing, traveling, and more can help you let go a bit while establishing new friendships and reinforcing old ones.

Be creative. Activating your creative side can help keep your brain healthy. Creativity can take many forms, from painting to gardening to teaching a child noun declensions in Latin. Tapping into creativity may also help you discover new parts of yourself.

Keep learning. Like being creative, ongoing learning keeps the mind active and the brain healthy. There are many ways to keep learning, from taking up a new language to starting—or returning to—an instrument you love, or exploring a subject that fascinates you.

Alright then, there you have it. There is more to your life than just looking forward to retirement. There is more to your life than for you to spend the later part of your life idling away somewhere in the name of retirement. In fact, true fulfillment in life is the result of a lifetime of active involvement in the fulfillment of a defined purpose.

So come along now and let's look into those specific tips you will need to live a satisfying, rewarding and fulfilling life.

PART 2:
Tips To Self-Fulfilment

Chapter 6

Don't Rest On Your Laurels

Chapter 6
Don't Rest On Your Laurels

You have put in efforts into becoming the very best in your field. You got the right educations. You worked harder than everybody else. You pushed yourself beyond the limit. You made the right connections and God crowned your efforts with success. Today, you are where your peers dreamt of being and you have the whole world at your feet. You have arrived. You know it and whole world does too. Kudos to you but newsflash! There is much more to your life than what you can see today.

There is a whole lot more in you to offer to your world. Where you are today is not the best that God planned for you. Where you are today is only a tip of the ice-berg regarding where you could be and what you could be doing. You are meant for something greater. There is a whole lot more embedded in you that you can offer to the world. Don't fall into the error of self-satisfaction because it is one of the greatest hindrances to self-fulfillment.

Self-satisfaction is the situation of being excessively satisfied with yourself while taking great pride in your achievements. It is the feeling of "arrival" after a significant accomplishment or feat. What is wrong with feeling satisfied after achieving something significant with my life you may ask? Well, there is nothing wrong with feeling satisfied from an achievement as long as it does not impede on your hunger and passion to go after more.

The problem with self-satisfaction at times is the fact that in most cases, it makes people feel like they have arrived. It makes people feel like they have gotten to their bus stop in life and so there is no need to press on and claim more grounds. It results in some form of complacency that is very difficult to deal with and I don't want that to happen to you. Don't let this be your story.

Don't allow yourself get to a point where you now feel like everything is okay and there is no need to press on. Otherwise, it becomes more difficult for you to put your best into whatever it is you are doing. And you know what that means; it means that you can never become better than who you are today. You cannot shoot past the level you have already attained. It's like placing an official ban on your own progress in life as you find yourself trapped within your comfort zone. This is the trap most high achieving people fall into.

The comfort zone is a big challenge in our generation today. Comfort zones create in us a sense of false fulfillment. They cause us to believe that we deserve to take a break and thereby place a limitation on us.

According to the dictionary the "comfort zone" described as the psychological state in which a person feels familiar, at ease, in control and experiences low anxiety and stress. Psychologists have been able to prove that optimal level of performance cannot be achieved within the comfort zone.

When you come to think of this it really does make sense. Think of a time when you had to get to the next level in your career or in something you were involved with. Think of a time when you had to take a new challenge to get further ahead in life. It must have tasked you mentally and physically but at the end of the day, because you pushed yourself so hard, you were able to come up with fantastic and amazing results that otherwise would not have been possible if you stayed within your comfort zone.

So, the best the comfort zone offers us is a steady level of performance but to get further ahead in life and reach your optimal performance, you've got to step out of your comfort zone.

"Life begins at the end of your comfort zone"

– Neale Donald Walsh

"We cannot become what we want to be by remaining what we are. We can only change our life, if we are brave enough to be out of our comfort zone. Because the first step to change in your circumstances is a change from within".

– Lou Macabasco.

Dangers Of Staying Within Your Comfort Zone

Comfort Zone Checkmates Your Growth In Life: Operating within your comfort zone creates a sense of false comfort and self-fulfillment. It makes you just content with where you are and what you have achieved. This makes it difficult for you to think outside the box and to stretch yourself in order to achieve extraordinary results. It makes you redundant and obsolete in an ever-changing world.

Comfort Zone Makes You Miss Opportunities In Life: Successful people are go-getters. They think outside the box and dare what the masses term as impossible. They are also on the look-out for opportunities and seize them with both hands when they spot them. They do not wait for things to happen rather they make things happen. That means that they don't operate within their comfort zones. If you will make the most of opportunities around then you've got to step out of your comfort zone.

Comfort Zone Causes Boredom And Lack Of Zest: When a man operates within his comfort zone, such a person is accustomed to routine. He is used to doing the same things over and over again. There is no excitement or thrill in his life. Before you know it, such a person will be filled with discontentment and dissatisfaction with his life. Every day will look the same for him because he is only doing the same things over and over again and therefore, he will only get the same results.

Staying Within Your Comfort Zone Can Trigger A Series Of Negative Emotions In You: This happens because while other people are busy getting their feet well, trying their best to get further in life, the man who is staying within his comfort zone is only going through the routines and motions of life. When the efforts of the other people who have been proactive begins to pay off, he of course has no result to show and thereby feelings of envy may well up within him and makes it even more difficult for him to succeed in life.

Comfort Zone Robs You Of Fulfillment In Life: To become fulfilled in life, you must become all that God has intended for you to be as well as fulfill all that He intended for you to be. A man who is operating within his comfort zone will definitely not be able to become all that God has intended for him to be. Neither will he be able to carry out all the assignment God has for him in this world hence he will never experience fulfillment in life.

Benefits Of Breaking Free From Your Comfort Zone

Haven seen some of the dangers of operating within your comfort zone, let us now look at the benefits of breaking free from your comfort zone.

You Will Become More Productive: Comfort zone and productivity are two parallel lines that can never meet. To be productive, you've got to keep on improving yourself, learn new things, improve your skills and push your personal boundaries. These are exactly the antithesis of comfort zone. Comfort zone zaps you of the much needed drive and ambition to become productive.

Living Outside Your Comfort Zone Helps You Prepare Adequately For Life's Unexpected Challenges: I like to say that life is predictable and success is predictable however that doesn't mean that things will always be smooth and rosy. There are certain circumstances that life throws in our path that we are not prepared for. For example the loss of something or someone dear to you.

Another example is that you might have to change your environment that you are familiar with in a scenario like war for instance and leave to an unfamiliar one. If you are the kind of person who has lived all his life hibernating in his comfort zone that means such occurrences might well mean the end of you. It may ruin you. It may even be for a good reason like getting a better job somewhere that

You have to transition. But if you are the kind of person that stays only within his comfort zone, it will prove really difficult for you. Operating out of your comfort zone however better prepares you to handle life's unexpected circumstances.

Stepping Out Of Your Comfort Zone Once Makes It Easier For You To Do So In The Future: Majority of the people you find around are accustomed to operating within their comfort zone. And why wouldn't they? When the comfort zone offers them a life of routine, security, warmth/comfort and even short-term fulfillment, it's only natural that they always want to stay there. But the moment, you take that bold step to start functioning outside your comfort zone as you push your boundaries, it only gets easier. Over time, you will discover that what would have sent a panic attack through you as you tried to attempt it before will become easier for you to do.

Operating Outside Your Comfort Zone Helps You To Fully Harness And Utilize All The Hidden Wealth And Potentials Stored Up In You: Venturing out of your comfort zone means you will be exposed to risks and unfamiliar circumstances. These circumstances will task your mind for solutions and answers. In bringing out these answers, you will inevitably get to discover some skills, ability, knowledge and strengths that you never knew you possessed. Operating outside your comfort zone forces you to dip into the amazing wealth you have on the inside. You never know how strong you are until you find yourself in the middle of a situation that calls for your strength to be tested.

It Gives You The Opportunity To Discover Yourself And Get To Know Yourself Better: Stepping your of your familiar zone means you will be trying new things. As you, do, you will discover things you could do that you never really knew all along. You will have a chance to discover your hidden strengths. You will also get to love yourself better. You essentially give yourself the opportunity to know, like and love yourself.

It Gives You The Opportunity To Meet New People That Could Make Tremendous Impact On Your Life: It's as simple as it sounds. While we tend to want to hide out in our familiar zones, we cannot get to meet new people. And in the world we live in now, making the right connections is one of the easiest and fastest way to advance in our careers and in life generally. Stepping out of your comfort zone will certainly bring you in contact with new people. Who knows maybe the person you have been looking for all your life to help you get further ahead in life, cause you to achieve your goals and even teach you new things might just be amongst the people you meet.

By Stepping Out Of Your Comfort Zone You Give Yourself The Opportunity To Succeed In Life: One of the many reasons that keeps people trapped in their comfort zone is fear. They are afraid that if they go out there and try new things then they would fail. In order not to fail they cling unto the safe haven that they have known all their lives. And they later wonder why they are not successful in life. The thing is that there can be no success or progress for the man who is not ready to risk failure. What is failure by the way? That you tried something and it didn't work out does not mean you failed or you are failure. It only means you've not found the right way to make it work and that is what you should direct your focus and attention to.

By the way, every time, you attempt something and fail at it, it only means you have found one way that thing will not work. The next time, you attempt the thing again, your experience the last time you failed will come in handy as an invaluable experience. Also, thought leaders have redefined the word "fail". They say it should be viewed as "first attempt in learning". I think that is brilliant.

Finally, Operating Outside Your Comfort Zone Will Help You To Keep Your Minds Sharp And Make You Age Better: A study released on October 21, 2013 reveals that when older people learn new and demanding skills while maintaining an engaged social network, they stay sharp and hence age better. The study was titled: The impact of sustained engagement on cognitive function in older adults" The research was championed by Denise Park, psychological scientist and lead researcher of the University of Texas at Dallas alongside some other colleagues. For their study, Park and colleagues randomly assigned 221 adult, ages 60 to 90, to engage in a particular type of activity for 15 hours a week over the course of three months.

Some participants were assigned to learn a new skill digital photography, quilting or both – which required active engagement and tapped working memory, long term memory and other high-level cognitive processes.

Other participants were instructed to engage in more familiar activities at home, such as listening to classical music and completing word puzzles. And to account for the possible influence of social contact, some participants were assigned to a social group that included social interactions, field trips and entertainment.

At the end of three months, Park and colleagues found that the adults who were productively engaged in learning new skills showed improvement in memory compared to those who engaged in social activities or non-demanding mental activities at home.

"The finding suggests that engagement alone is not enough" says Park. The three learning groups were pushed very hard to keep learning more and mastering more tasks and skills. Only the groups that were confronted with continuous and prolonged mental challenge improved. Essentially, it was only the groups that stepped out of their comfort zone experienced a marked improvement in their cognitive functioning. This has given rise to a speculation that operating outside the comfort zone could slow the rate at which the brain ages. Should this prove true, the implication is that even as people advance in years the quality of their lives will not reduce and they can still live an independent life.

How to break free of your comfort zone

Hang Out With Risk Takers: A man eventually becomes like the company he keeps. Hang out with people who are daring and are accustomed to taking risks. Eventually, their attitude will rub off on you and influence you to do same.

Break Up Your Routine And Try New Things Occasionally: It could be something as simple as changing the route you take to work every day or the route you take your school or even the gym. It could also mean reading a different kind of book apart from the one you normally read e.g. if you're mostly a non-fiction reader, then you could try out fiction. The bottom line is change your everyday routine frequently and do things differently.

Identify The Things That Are Outside Your Comfort Zone And Start Tackling Them One After The Other: Each person's comfort zone is unique to him. One person may be afraid of speaking in the public so he avoids it at all cost. Another person may be afraid of failure and as a result shies away from daring new things. So, everybody has their own comfort zone and things that lie outside their comfort zone. Get familiar with the things that lies outside your comfort zone and start reaching out to do them one after the other.

Take It One Step At A Time: Breaking free of your comfort zone does not have to be a rushed event instead take it slowly. Start out slowly because things may not always work out as you planned and the temptation to rush back into your comfort zone is always around the corner. Taking the theme of public speaking for example, you don't have to rush right on stage the first time if it's out of your comfort zone. Instead you can take your time to start talking to small groups of people and increase the circle over time as you prepare yourself to face a larger audience someday.

Focus On All The Potential Good And Benefits That Could Come From Being Outside Your Comfort Zone: When you want to attempt things that are unfamiliar to you and outside your comfort zone, you will come up with doubts such as; what if it doesn't work out?, what if people make fun of me?. Well, when those thoughts plague you, counter them with thoughts of positivity. So, you turn the table on the thoughts and ask; what if it works out? What if everything turns out well?, what if it inspires other people?. Then go for it. You know what, at the end of the day, even if things don't go like you planned for them to go, you would have had an experience out of just trying whatever it is you tried. An experience that will come in handy for you in the future because no knowledge gained is lost. Most importantly, the fulfillment of doing that thing will be yours.

Physical standards does not determine our fulfillment

Sometimes we use physical standards to determine our fulfillments. Some people think if they could have a family with a number of cars, a house and a nice paying job, then they would be fulfilled. This is a false comfort. Some other people think they would be fulfilled if they could finish their education and get a nice paying job.

"No man can begin to mold himself on a faith or an idea without rising to a higher order of experience."

- George Eliot

All these aspirations are what keep us self-satisfied. That false feeling of self-fulfillment deprives us of the future we could have. It robs us of the energy that could be put into generating new ideas and pursuing their fulfillment. Physical parameters like a job, family status, salary, don't equate to self-fulfillment.

Fulfillment of self is much greater than attaining a status in society. It's much greater than a comfortable life style. Self-fulfillment is much greater than seeing your children and grandchildren. Self-fulfillment is greater than what could be measured physically or materially.

Chapter 7

Don't Compare
Yourself To Others

Chapter 7
Don't Compare Yourself To Others

Now that you understand how not to sit on your laurels because there is much more to be done, lets take it a step further down the lane of the tips to self-fulfillment, it's time to get those comparisons out of the way!

"Comparison is a thug that robs your joy. But it's even more than that - Comparison makes you a thug who beats down somebody - or your soul."

- Ann Voskamp

Way too many people make the grave mistake of comparing themselves to others in their walk and journey of life. Too many end u stopping by the way side on the path to achievements because they compare themselves with other people. I must add however, that you shouldn't make the mistake to think that people only compare themselves with those who they think are better than themselves but a lot of people also compare themselves to those whom they think they are worse than. This is a very dangerous kind of comparison because it is a harbinger to a man's progress in life.

Now, let's explore the subject of comparing yourself with other people. Social psychologist Leon Festinger was the one who proposed the theory of social comparison in the year 1954.

This theory is centered on the belief that every human being possesses a drive for accurate self-evaluation. Naturally, people want to evaluate their abilities, opinions and skills. The theory proves that people compare themselves to other individuals when they want to gain an accurate evaluation on their own abilities and opinions. Doing this gives them a sense of a sense of validity and cognitive clarity in defining self.

Festinger's theory was well researched by Wills, Baumeister and some other people. These made them come up with two different kinds of comparison that people generally make.

1) Downward comparison

2) Upward comparison

Downward comparison

happens when an individual compares himself with others who are worse off than him. For example, a student who scored 60% in a test comparing himself to another one who scored 29%.

Two types of downward comparison were also identified.

The first is the passive downward comparison where an individual takes into consideration a previous condition and bases his comparison on that. For example, the student who compares himself with another student who had a lower percentage. He was not the cause of the other student's poor performance. He only got to know about it and in order to feel good with his own performance, he made a comparison.

However, an active downward comparison occurs when a person compares himself to others by actively causing harm to them or making demeaning and derogatory remarks about them. For those who engage in active downward comparison, they cause harm to the person they are trying to compare themselves to so that they can create a situation where such people will be worse off than they are and therefore they will have the proper opportunity to make the comparison they are trying to make. Also demeaning and making derogatory remarks about the person affords them the opportunity to place an even greater distance between themselves and the person they are trying to compare themselves to.

Many of us try to feel good about ourselves by looking at those who we consider to be worse than us. While it could be a temporary solace, it is never a good solution.

Of course, if you look around enough, you will always find people who are doing worse than you. But what does that achieve for you? At the most, probably, it will help you to feel like a local hero but that kind of practice doesn't help you to become all that God wants you to be. It will serve to place an embargo on your journey towards fulfillment in life. It makes you relax in your efforts to reach higher and aim for more. It also makes you complacent and content with who you are and what you have already done. It closes your mind to ideas and inspirations that could have better enhanced your life. Therefore, in order to come to know fulfillment in your life, this is a golden rule that you should never compromise on. That is, never you compare yourself with others whom you perceive to be doing worse than you are.

How about upward comparison? Is it a better kind of comparison to make? Let's see.

Definition - Upward comparison happens when an individual compares himself with others who are better than him. For example an upcoming actor comparing himself with a veteran who has won an Oscar.

Yes, there are cases when comparing yourself with those better than you could inspire you and encourage you to do better. As nice and as cool as that sounds, what happens when you don't have such individuals around you to emulate? Even though it is a nice idea to have a model before you, whose height you aspire to, yet the greatest motivation should be what is coming from within you.

While it may seem that upward comparison is a better alternative to downward comparison, it is not always so. Research has proven that making upward comparison may serve as a source of motivation to help us push our boundaries in order to become more like the person we are comparing ourselves to. But, generally it makes us feel bad and inadequate. It makes us feel like every other person is doing well about ourselves. It could be paralyzing, demoralizing and at the same time debilitating and thus we should not compare ourselves with others.

And oh, the social media world does not help at all. Different posts come up on Facebook, twitter and Instagram about how other people's lives are shining and sparkling but what we don't realize is that the status updates and pictures people put about themselves on social media are the very best aspects of their lives.

They don't put their struggles, tears, fears, shame, embarrassment and challenges on Facebook. Oh, they don't put the fact that they are going through a turbulent time in their marriages up. They don't post pictures of themselves struggling to quit a habit. They don't post updates about the debts they are struggling to pay up. Even for something as simple as baring their natural face unmade up for all to see, they wouldn't post.

Instead, they post these pictures and updates about a perfect life that doesn't exist anyway but it throws your own world into absolute disarray causing you to feel inadequate and less than good.

«The reason why we struggle with insecurity is because we compare our behind the scenes with everyone else's highlight reel.»

-Steve Furtick

And to wrap it up with Theodore Roosevelt's words; comparison steals our joy.

Debby was an upcoming musician who moved to the city of Nashville to sing. She went to the prestigious Belmont University for Music Business. So, naturally she thought she would learn the music business while performing on the side. However, when she got there, everyone else was doing the same. That started her out on the dangerous route of comparing herself to all the girls who had sweeter, stronger and «better» voices than her.

Also, she made observations of other people were able to write their own songs, play all kinds of instruments and suddenly she formed this notion about herself that she wasn't as much of a musician as she thought in comparison to others. She was comparing herself to others that she thought better than herself.

In no time, while her fellow students were busy forming their own bands, going for song contests and winning prizes, even putting together press kits for their songs. Debby could no longer start and finish writing her songs anymore because she became worried that she wasn't wasn't good enough and every other person would laugh at her. Before long she stopped performing. Couldn't practice anymore and generally lost hope that she could ever be successful as a musician.

She felt like she didn't know who she was anymore because all the while she was comparing herself to others. Few months' later students from the same school as she was - Belmont University, have record deals and have their music all over different music channels but in her own case she has managed to become irrelevant in the music world.

This is exactly what comparing yourself to others does to you. It robs you of the valuable time you can put into developing yourself and making giant strides towards the future of your dreams. Statistically, every human being has 86,400 seconds to himself in a day. It is up to you what to do with each of these precious seconds. But imagine that you spend every single one of them profitably on activities and exercises that will inch you several steps closer to your goal rather than wasting them trying to measure how you stack up against other people's achievements and successes in life.

Frankly, self-comparison is not only a thief of joy but it is also a thief of time. That's not all still. For Debby above, she pointed out that it got to a time when she felt like she didn't even know who she was anymore.

Ouch, this is another dangerous side effect of comparing yourself to others. It literally robs you of your self-identity. It shifts your focus away from self to others. It makes you see yourself through the lenses of the other person's eyes. That is, instead of focusing on yourself and what you want for your of life, you are focused on this other person/people you're comparing yourself to, trying to become like them, trying to do what they are doing and trying to achieve what they have achieved.

In this process of trying to become like them, you will begin to lose your own uniqueness, identity, sense of self and eventually you will lose your self-esteem. You will lose your self-esteem because you will only become the shadow of this person. Losing yourself in this manner also makes you lose your direction and purpose for life. Since, instead of having your own goals in focus, you have adopted another man's life cum goal.

Another reason not to compare yourself with others is because it leads to resentment and bitterness.

Comparison leads to resentment and bitterness because after trying your best all your life to become like them and achieve what they have achieved but you fail, the only natural emotion that will well in you will be anger, envy and jealousy. This will cause you to harbor resentment towards them.

So, whichever way, you look at comparison either downward or upward, none of them is healthy for you and none will lead to the path of self-fulfillment.

The next time you are tempted to compare yourself with others, remind yourself of these words by Justin Zoradi:

"They have their story and I have mine. They have their story and I have mine. They have their story..."

- Justin Zoradi

Also remember this quotation by an unknown author

"Why compare yourself with others? No one in the entire world can do a better job of being you than you."

In moving ahead, while many thought leaders generally agree with the fact that comparing ourselves with others is detrimental to our success in life, they however embrace the idea that comparing ourselves with what we have done in the past is the holy grail of success. In effect, they are of the opinion that instead of comparing yourself with other people, you should only compare yourself to yourself as well as compare yourself with your past achievements.

For example what are you doing today that you weren't doing 3,4,5 years ago? Or what are your wins this year compared to this time last year? In other words how have you improved today compared with your past self? As logically sound as this argument is what if what you achieved this year is what you were meant to have achieved 5 years ago.

That means you will only feel good and gratified falsely because you inaccurately estimated yourself. It may make you feel like you are doing well but in reality this is wrong because what you are counting as doing well today is what you were meant to have achieved 5 years ago. So, logically speaking, you are like 5 years behind but you are not seeing it and this is self-limiting in itself.

Therefore the right comparison for us to make is not against what we have already done.

What we should compare ourselves against

Instead our goal should be to compare ourselves with the potential God has put in us. We should really only compare ourselves with our calling, mission and potential

Our race is against the mandate of God upon our lives. There is an expectation that God has for your life. Have you discovered it? Do you know why you are here on planet earth? Have you started fulfilling your purpose for this world?

These are the questions that should continuously run through your mind and these are the things you should strive to accomplish. You should look for God's expectation of you and strive to fulfill it.

You are uniquely unique and so is your purpose. There is a reason why God made you the way you are and gave you all the ability and skills, potentials, talents and all that you find working in your life today. It is so that you might fulfill some specific tasks and assignment on earth. And you will never be able to fulfill them by constantly looking over your shoulders at what everybody else has got and what they are all doing.

It is in this same manner that God created all the different parts of the body with some being one, others two and some others like our fingers 10 and He placed them at different locations depending on what their functions were supposed to be. Just imagine that instead of your eyes being two, they are ten and littered all around your head, how will you look like?

Okay, imagine that instead of hairs been on your head, your intestines are the ones hanging on your head, how nice will that look? The point we are making here is that God created all the different parts of the body with a specific assignment and purpose in mind so, it will be wrong for your tongue instead to keep looking over its shoulders desiring that it looks like your nose and performs the function of smell.

It is in this manner that God made you uniquely and made your purpose unique to you. Find this purpose and fulfill it to the best of God's ability in you. Determine in your heart that you will be the best in the area God has gifted you to serve this world. Make sure you fully utilize your potentials. Become the best version of you.

Reign and rule in your sector, domain and area of influence. This is the best comparison you can do for yourself.

Wouldn't it interest you to know that in all the 4.5 billion years the earth has existed for, there has been nobody like you who walked the face of this earth and there will be no other person like you who will walk this earth. You are the rarest and the most unique of your kind. Don't throw this away in a bid to become like another person as you compare yourself. God has given you everything within you to be complete in yourself. He has filled you up with abilities, skill, talents, wealth of potentials that are necessary to take you to the zenith in life. It's time for you to maximize all you've got to the fullest.

"Try not to get lost in comparing yourself to others. Discover your gifts and let them shine!"

- Jennie Finch

Rather than getting lost in the see of the crowd all in the name of comparison, why don't you discover your gifts and life assignment then go all out to be the best in your field? You will always find that fulfillment in life is the direct result of a life that is fulfilling its purpose and calling rather than one that is all about catching up with others.

"Within you, you will find everything you need to be complete."

\- Bryant McGill

"Strive to become the best version of your original self. That's where your true fulfillment in life lies."

\- Edmond Mbiaka

Chapter 8

You Can't Change What You Can Tolerate

Chapter 8
You Can't Change What You Can Tolerate

One of the beauties of life is the fact that you are the one who gets to decide what becomes of your life. You are the one who gets to decide how far you go and what your outcomes will be. As a matter of fact, it is impossible for anyone and anything to come in the way of your fulfillment in life without your express permission. It is just sad that many people give that permission without even knowing it

If you truly want to come to self-fulfillment, be careful of those things you tolerate or allow in your life. If you tolerate friends who waste your time, you might never be able to easily get rid of them nor regain the time you lose to them. If you tolerate TV and TV programs, that might become a menace and you might never be able to overcome it. If you tolerate empty, meaningless chat on the telephone, you will discover that it will become more and more difficult for you to stop. If you tolerate laziness, you will find it more difficult to break out of it. If you tolerate substandard quality, you will not be able to break out of that circle.

If you refuse to take the initiative but tolerate that others decide your future and your destiny, you will find it almost impossible to be able to make your own decisions. If you tolerate drinking and smoking, you will become addicted to them. If you tolerate day dreaming and empty fantasies, those things will stand in the way of your self-fulfillment.

If you tolerate excuses, they will become a way of life for you and serve to ruin your future and destiny. If you tolerate gossip, it will destroy the purity of your heart and turn you to a channel for causing social damage. If you tolerate lies, you will live a dishonest life, come under its dominion and you will never be able to come to self-fulfillment.

If you tolerate self-condemnation, it will destroy your self-esteem, make you think low of yourself and sabotage your chances at self-fulfillment. And if you tolerate fear, it will make you live in a cocoon where you are afraid and unable to rise up and take daring and bold steps that will bring you closer to self-fulfillment.

Someone might be saying, "How can anyone who is serious about his life tolerate all these". That definitely can't happen to me. But what you have to understand is that refusal to choose one option or path in life is an automatic decision in favor of the other. The moment you refuse to neglect making the right choices for your life, you have automatically made the wrong one. This is exactly how many found themselves in the wrong places in life. So you have to become proactive and take a stand for your life.

As a matter of fact, what we tolerate, we empower. What we tolerate, we enthrone. Tolerating something means giving up some of your power. Tolerating means giving up your resistance. Tolerating is refusing to resist. Tolerating is an unwillingness to fight or oppose something. That is why it becomes incredibly difficult and almost impossible to change those things we tolerate.

When you tolerate things you actually give them the permission to exact a measure of authority over you. However, that limited authority could easily become a fully-fledged dominion over you, if you tolerate it long enough. In that case, what we tolerate does not only become extremely difficult to change, but worse still what we tolerate often has dominion over us.

"You are the only real obstacle in your path to a fulfilling life."

- Les Brown

For example a person that gives himself to smoking once in a while, would soon discover that he has come under its power, resulting in addiction. A person who allows himself the pleasure of sometimes watching pornography, would soon discover that he practically cannot stop doing it any longer. That is total dominion because of a little permission given.

So ladies and gentlemen, if you wish to be fulfilled in life, there are some things you don't want to tolerate or permit. There are certain things you don't want to give a chance at all. Those things you permit will either stop your fulfillment or enhance your fulfillment. So be careful about those things you permit in your life.

Lucas was a junk food eater who did not discriminate against anything fried, sugary or baked. At just 27 years of age, he was already approaching the three hundred pound mark with lightning speed. He had always been fat but this was his highest weight of all times. Of course such a weight came with its medical complications. Part of which includes ankle and feet ache, shortness of breath, severe acid reflux, blood pressure problems, sleep apnea and all the other unpleasant side effects associated with being morbidly obese.

In addition to the medical problems that he was grappling with, Lucas also had to squeeze myself into his car seat, could barely tie his own shoes, was constantly unable to find clothes that were his sizes in the clothing stores and to make matters worse, his weight was about to make him lose his job and send him into the dog eat dog labor market.

Lucas was a marketing consultant and part of his duties includes working closely with the higher management of his company as well as interviewing employees from time to time and making them answer questions related to the company. He also organized seminars and events as well as interact with the media for press releases that will boost the company's image.

In essence, Lucas role was such that required him coming in contact with a lot of people from time to time. Since first impression matters people tended not to take him for the professional that he was when they saw the unhealthy pounds he had packed on and his employers were seriously beginning to have a rethink as to why they hired him in the first instance. Somebody whispered the conversation going on among the management to him and this served as some sort of wake-up call for him.

Before then, one of Lucas's favorite quote had been:

"You can't change what you can tolerate!"

But he never really attached any significance to it until his source of livelihood felt threatened! It was then that he realized that he had indeed reached the point where he could no longer tolerate the excessive pounds he had packed on. He also realized that he could no longer tolerate the discomfort and accompanying misery that his weight had brought upon him.

His decisions led him to go scour the internet for any information that could help him on his journey to losing weight and keeping fit. It wasn't easy for him at the beginning as there were a lot of information on dieting and exercising out there and he had to find the specific ones that will cater to his needs and help him achieve his goals of being fit and healthy. After much trials and error, sweat and tears he dropped to his desired weight - a healthy 178 pounds.

You may want to examine your life today and ask yourself certain questions. What are those things that cause you pain, shame or embarrassment? What are those things that have introduced discomfort into your life and those things that are sabotaging your progress, success and happiness in life? What are the things that you have permitted and you have given excuses for all these years and come to accept as being permanent residents in your life?

It is time to take a stand, put your foot down and affirm to yourself "enough is enough" in your life. It's time to reclaim the steering wheel of your life from all those things that you have permitted to run and control your life and have now become a stumbling block on your path to self-fulfillment.

You must rise up to take responsibility for your life. Don't be fooled, no habit, situation, circumstance or even human being has the right to Lord it over your life. You are the one to call the shots in your life. You decide what you want to stay in your life and what you want to leave. Don't even give yourself the permission to think that things are the way they are in your life because they were meant to be. No that is a victim's thought. You are not a victim, you are an emperor, a lord in your own class.

You should be in control of your own life and in control of what happens to you. So, rather than think that things are the way they are in your life because they are meant to be, think instead on the fact that things are the way they are in your life because you allowed them to be.

Like Lucas, the day, you discover those things that are sabotaging your happiness and limiting your chances to come to self-fulfillment that is the day you must rise to take up action and do all you have to do to eliminate those things in your life. And the place to begin from to make this happen is to get informed on what you should do right away.

Go to the professionals, let them equip you with the right knowledge to start changing what you must to attain self-fulfillment. For example, maybe you've found yourself in bad debt because over the years you have tolerated accumulation of debt. It's no problem, now that your eyes are opened and you are unwilling to tolerate the sleepless nights that the debts are causing you, the first thing you want to do is to go to your accountant and explore every possible solution out of the debt with him.

The same thing applies to every area of life. Maybe it's your marriage going through the storm and you have tolerated an unhealthy marriage for a long time but you are unwilling to keep on tolerating it, then you might want to go to a marriage counselor, seek his opinion and let him help you with guidelines on how to start restoring bliss in your home.

There is information and better still a professional who can help you out of any dilemma you might have found yourself in, seek them out. Don't just sit and lament and accept that the way things are in your life is final. You've got a part to play. The moment you make up your mind not to accept that thing any longer and you start taking commensurate actions to change the situation, you will find that things will begin to take a turn in the positive for you.

There is this old English proverb that says "where there is a will, there is a way"

"Intolerance of your present creates your future"

– Mike Murdock.

Don't settle for any less than you can have. Don't resign to fate about what you can become or what is possible with you. Push, push again and push some more. And let these words of Mike Murdock ring in your mind. You are only qualified for the future when you become intolerant of the resent!

Now, rather than sitting there lamenting over what has happened in the past because of your negligence, I want you to take a different approach. Complaining about what you have permitted before now won't change anything. What you should do instead is to sit down, find out where it is you gave out that permission then simply begin to withdraw it.

The moment you identify those things you have permitted in your life that aren't necessarily leading to the kind of results you want in life, you are delivered! Your fulfillment and satisfaction in life is connected to your ability identify these things you tolerate and withdrawing your permissions.

Chapter 9

Crisis Are Not Tragedies, They Are Traffic Lights

Chapter 9
Crisis Are Not Tragedies, They Are Traffic Lights

Many people have failed to be fulfilled in life simply because they encountered some form of crisis or difficulty. Many have missed out on what could have otherwise been a fulfilling life because they didn't understand what crisis really are and how to respond to them.

One story particularly stands out in my mind of someone who gave up just before his dreams, hopes and aspirations were realized. Just at the verge of success Tommy gave up on what could have been an otherwise fulfilling life. Tommy was an only child whose parents were busy professionals. His dad was an investment banker and his mum, a nurse. During Tommy's growing up days, he hardly ever saw them at home as his mum had to work both day and night, including weekends in some cases. His dad also had to leave for work early every morning and often worked on the weekends too.

Tommy therefore had to spend a lot of time with his grandma who looked after him while his parents were away. In trying to make up for their lack of availability of time with Tommy, His parents often squeezed out time to take him to the cinema or to restaurants just so they could spend some family time together. These frequent visits to the cinema made Tommy develop a love for movies so much so that he applied to the University to study theatre arts.

He was a good student by every definition of the word. Just as he was rounding up his studies at the University, Tommy had a brilliant idea to make a film that would not only entertain people but will inspire them as well. The whole idea of the movie was to get across to different famous and successful people in different fields of life and get their stories out of them.

On his list of people to meet, he had billionaires who rose from humble backgrounds and had to work their way to the top. Also he had some famous actors, musicians, TV personalities and even the president of his nation on that list.

His aim was to meet diverse successful people from all across the world, listen to their story of success and whip all of these together into a movie that will inspire the hearts of millions.

So, the first thing he did was to go to the Dean of Faculty in his school. In an animated conversation, he shared the idea with the Dean. Unfortunately, the dean believed in him and in his vision but that was where it ended.

He simply told him that the school did not have the necessary finances to embark on such a grandiose project moreover the people he had on his "to meet list" were way out of his league and there was just no way they could make contacts with them.

This hurt Tommy badly but he decided not to give up on his dreams so, he went to meet a wealthy uncle of his who resided in Russia for help. Again, he met with a brick wall there as the uncle didn't buy into the project.

Tommy then thought to himself that maybe all he needed was to get a large amount of money to film but as for the contacts he needed to make, he would get to the people directly by himself. He didn't have the resources needed but he scoured the internet to look for organizations that allowed people to showcase their talents in order to qualify for sponsorship. He found quite a lot and he submitted his proposal to them one after the other so that they could help with financing his movie. Many of them admitted that the submission was brilliant however they were not looking to investing into such a project as at that time. Time was running out fast and Tommy was beginning to get a little frustrated.

One day, he ran into a childhood friend in whom he confided in on challenges he was facing. Haven't heard all he said the friend advised him to stop hunting for money but rather channel his energy towards contacting the influential people whose story he was going to turn into the movie. Buttressing his point with the fact that the money for production wasn't the first thing he needed but the script for the movie itself.

That sparked something up in Tommy and he decided to do just that. He set to work immediately and drafted out the mails he was going to send around to the respective offices and secretaries of the influencers.

He had high hopes and expectations. He needed to feature only 12 people in the movie but he wrote to about a 60 of them just to increase his chances of actually getting across to some of them.

Oh! Tommy worked hard for what he believed was going to inspire and motivate a lot of people to dream big and reach for their dreams. Day after day, he sent the mails to the respective offices and even went ahead to lay hold of as many phone numbers of the secretary in a bid to get them to set up an appointment for him.

"The road to success for 99% of the people isn't a jump! It is a steady incline!"

-Lee Morris

This couldn't have been truer in Tommy's case. Day after day, he picked up his phone in a bid to confirm his appointment but to his disappointment, he only met with rejection.

The time was flying by fast and the little resources he had for surviving and taking care of his family was fast dwindling. Also, he had become a laughing stock amongst his friends and some had even parted ways with him, calling him a failure. But, somehow he persevered and kept going because he believed so much in the power of his project.

Sometimes he got appointments set up only for it to be postponed for as much as 30 times after which he was eventually turned down.

On some other occasions, he would be asked to come to a certain location with his camera crew so that he could get on with the interview. At such times, he had to hire the crew he needed only to get to the agreed location to discover that it was all a fib, there was no one in sight, neither the secretary nor the important personality he was looking forward to meeting.

The last straw that broke the Carmel's back for him was when the secretary of a real estate billionaire called him from the United States to tell him that the appointment was all good and set up. Ordinarily Tommy should have been exhilarated by this news. However, he received it with mixed feelings. On one hand, he was excited about finally getting an appointment set up that was confirmed by the secretary that called him.

On the other hand, his wife was pregnant with their first child and was at the tail end of her pregnancy. As a matter of fact, she had checked into the hospital awaiting the baby's arrival and the arrival coincided with the time the appointment was set up for. Tommy lived far-away South Africa and couldn't see himself leaving his wife to the delivery all by herself. After much deliberation with his wife they agreed that he could go which he did.

On the said day of the interview, he got to the office of the billionaire mogul with high expectations and a sense of victory that at last, his dreams of producing his movie was about to come to pass. But his joy was short-lived when the secretary told him that the billionaire had cancelled out at the last minute.

His pleas about the fact that he had to travel all the way from South Africa to the US with his wife being in the hospital to deliver their child all fell on deaf ears. The meeting was cancelled and there was to be no change in the decision was all the secretary said.

Tommy was furious as he grabbed the secretary and gave her the shake of her life. But of course, that did nothing to change the state of things. With a heavy heart, he returned back home to discover that his wife had delivered their baby in his absence. That did little to brighten his heart because all the resources they could have used to take care of the baby for the first few weeks and months of life had gone down the drain with the trip he made.

The coming days and weeks saw Tommy sinking into a depression. He had no motivation nor zest for life again. He quitted his search of meeting the celebrities and spent his days sleeping, cursing and making life unbearable for his wife at home. His nights, he spent wandering from pub to pub hoping to seek relieve from alcohol. 6 months after his trip home from the United States, he decided to turn on his computer and read his mails. There were a total of 184 mails in his inbox and approximately 100 of them was sent from the office of Oprah Winfrey!

It so happened that Oprah was one of the people he had written to requesting for an interview with her. In the months when he was suffering from his bouts of depression, her people had gotten back to him requesting for him to come over because she was ready to meet with him but they couldn't get across to him. They sent him several mails and he responded to none of them.

They even requested for his bank account details so they could transfer the sum of money necessary to cover his travel expenses and yet he didn't respond because he didn't see his mails. Finally, Oprah had a world women's leader conference in South Africa where she was going to be speaking. Again, her office tried to contact Tommy to find out whether he was free to have the interview with her in South Africa; but once more there was no Tommy.

By the time he eventually saw the mails, the last one that was sent to him from her office was already 2 months old.

He feverishly rushed to contact her office again but there was no response forth-coming. He sent one mail after the other but they generated no reply and he became overcame with grief.

How true it is that the darkest hour of the night is just before dawn. Only, if he had not succumbed to the pressure of failure just at the brink of success, definitely his meeting with Oprah would have made his dreams of shooting his movie a reality. Because, once he got Oprah on the team, he could be sure to get many more others but he quitted just at the verge of success.

Where exactly are you at this point in your life? What are you pursuing with all your might that seems elusive to you? This is not the time to throw in the towel and give up on your dreams. You must keep pushing and keep pressing hard because your glory might just be around the corner. Give it one more shot and then another and another until your hands lay hold on the pursuit that you are after.

Friends let's face it, there is no one that would ever come to fulfillment or any great height in life without encountering challenges, problems, difficulties and crises. Problems are a part of life. The faster we get used to that thought the better it will be for us.

Problems are not meant to stop you on your way to progress. They are there to propel you forward. How many dreams have died just because difficulties arose on the way?

How many projects have been abandoned because some problems arose in the path of pursuing them? Too many destinies are cut short of their best, because troubles arose in their paths.

That is why we must be conscious enough of the fact that crises don't come to stop us.

"Every adversity, every failure, every heartache carries with it the seed on an equal or greater benefit."

– Napoleon Hill

One of the most constructive ways of maximizing crises to our benefit is to look at them as traffic lights. In life sometimes, situations arise that are like red lights to us. At such times we know we must have a temporary stoppage and we must allow some things to come to pass before we again possess the permission to move forward at full speed.

At other times, it is a yellow light that we encounter. These are crises, challenges and troubles that don't entirely stop us but slow us down and they also have their own benefits. Interestingly some crises in life might actually be a green light. As paradoxical as that might sound; we pass through different circumstances in life that at first glance look like unpleasant trouble. However in the long run, these circumstances could actually work out for our good, thereby becoming a green light for our acceleration in life.

The story of Sylvester Stallone

During his birth, the doctor taking his delivery performed a wrong gynecological procedure that caused Stallone to have paralysis in the lower left side of his face – including parts of his lip, tongue and chin. This made his face have a permanent snarl-like look to it. Also, when he spoke, his speech was slightly slurred. To make matters worse, at school, the other pupils made fun of him because of his paralysis.

This forced him to start body-building because he wanted to both defend himself and frighten away those who bullied him. In the course of his body-building adventure he took a liking to the movie industry and wanted so badly to become an actor.

Around 1974, his wife got pregnant and all Sylvester possessed included a dog that he loved a lot, many bills that needed to be paid and absolutely no success in his movie career but then he also had a rock solid belief in his dream that he was going to make it big in life.

Soon a time came when he went flat broke and was heavily indebted.

Things got so bad that he had to sell his wife's jewelries and in no time they were kicked out of their home and thereby becoming homeless.

His desperate situation forced him to take a hard decision that led to him parting with his dog. This was the same dog he had earlier risked his life to save at a wild life reserve. The dog had been attacked by a wild ostrich who was bent on pecking the dog to death. Instead of Stallone to protect himself and get out of harm's way, he jumped out of his car and went after the two animals. In the process of trying to get his dog away from the ostrich, the ostrich turned on him and began to peck him instead but he managed to save his dog. However, when his condition got really bad, he sold the same dog for a paltry sum of money.

Two weeks after that, he watched a boxing match between Mohammed Ali and Chuck Weppner. Mohammed Ali was practically slaughtering Weppner in that match but Weppner refused to give up. Every time, he was thrown to the ground, he kept rising back to fight even though his chances of winning were slim. That match was like a flash of inspiration to Stallone as it motivated him to write his first movie script to become an instant hit. He actually wrote out the whole script in a notebook in just 20 hours.

When the script was completed, he went from one movie studio to the other with the aim of getting them to buy the script and cast him as the male lead role in the movie. But this was not to be so because in that era movie stars were supposed to be super handsome men who spoke fluently. And here was a body builder with a facial paralysis that caused him to stammer while speaking wanting to become a movie star. To many observers Stallone was simply a joker.

After nearly 1500 rejections, he got a production house to offer $125,000 for the script. You would have thought Stallone would accept the offer with both arms and feet thrown wide open but he didn't simply because they wanted only the script and not him for the lead role.

Despite the poverty, pains, pregnant wife and his sold dog, he didn't accept the offer. His dream was to be the star of the movie and he wouldn't budge otherwise. He wasn't willing to take anything than what he had desired in his heart.

A few weeks later, the studio called him up and this time they offered him $250,000 for the script and not him. Once again, he refused. Soon they offered $350,000 for the script but once more he declined.

At that point everyone thought he was mad for refusing such a mouth-watering offer. All his friends and family tried pushing him to accept the offer but his position remained unyielding.

Eventually, mother luck smiled on him as someone in the studio really loved his script and proposed to him the sum of $35,000 for the script but he would also be cast as the lead star. The rest as they say is history!

The movie was made for $1 million and went to gross around $225 million in global box office receipts, becoming the highest grossing film of 1976 . The movie also won 3 Oscars – Best Picture, Best Direction and Best Film Editing.

Also the film received many positive reviews and turned Stallone into a "bankable" hero for the next 20yrs, till the late 90s… with his movies making billions of dollars.

40 years have gone by since he wrote that movie but today ROCKY is still as much popular as it was in the year 1976. And what did he do with the first $35,000?

He went back to meet the person he had earlier sold his dog to and bought the dog back for an undisclosed amount of money.

In the words of Sylvester Stallone –

"Let me tell you something you already know. The world ain't all sunshine and rainbows. It's a very mean and nasty place and I don't care how tough you are it will beat you to your knees and keep you there permanently if you let it. You, me, or nobody is gonna hit as hard as life. But it ain't about how hard ya hit. It's about how hard you can get hit and keep moving forward. How much you can take and keep moving forward. That's how winning is done!"

- Sylvester Stallone, Rocky

Dear friends; the thing is this what was meant to act as a crisis in Sylvester Stallone's life later turned out to be the very thing that brought him success, wealth and fulfillment. The partial paralysis on his face that ought to have served as a hindrance to fulfilling his purpose in life led him down the route of building his body in order to scare off bullies who were constantly making fun of his physical looks. It was in the course of this body-building that he developed a love for acting in movies and found his fulfillment in life thereafter.

Probably, if that medical mistake was not made, he might never have considered building his body to the point of starring in movies and he would never have known the success and fulfillment that he had come to know in his life. It is the same thing for you today. Who knows, just maybe some of the crises you are going through right now are what will eventually lead you to your place of fulfillment. Peradventure, your "not so palatable" situation today is what will eventually be your steppingstone into success, glory, wealth and fulfillment. I am convinced that most of us will eventually have to look back and thank God for some of our crises.

At times crisis might be used by God to remove us from the mediocrity of life. In other words challenges, problems, troubles and crises come, so that we don't remain as we are today. They come to challenge and nudge us to bring out our best and do much more than we ordinarily would.

They could act as wakeup calls for us; preventing us from dropping into a relaxed mode in our pursuit of self-fulfillment. When we remain in the same place for too long because we are enjoying the comfort of it, we can never become our future.

Crisis Can ALSO Be Used To Lead Us Into New Discoveries, New Horizons And New Inventions.

If you always do the same thing over and again, you will most likely not get any new results in your life. You will only get the same old results you are used to getting and that can really be boring.

"Sometimes you need a little crisis to get your adrenaline flowing and help you realize your potential."

- Jeannette Walls.

Most of us never know what we can really do until we are put to the test. And in most cases, the best way to be put to the test is to find yourself in a situation that requires you to act. Finding yourself in a situation that challenges your creativity is the best way to express you full potentials.

In order to achieve new heights, we have to do new things. We have to take on new challenges to conquer so that we can have new victories. Therefore crises, circumstances and problems will often come into our lives as an instrument in the hand of God to move us out of mediocrity and into our destiny.

Every good student sees examination period as a time that precedes promotion and not a time for unjust judgment. You too should begin to see your times of crises as a prelude to your next level in life.

Chapter 10

Faith Is Inevitable

Chapter 10
Faith Is Inevitable

Now that you understand the role and importance of crisis as well as how to use them as stepping-stones to attain self-fulfillment, the stage is set for yet another very important tip for self-fulfillment in life. This time around, we are going to be looking at the subject of faith.

But really, what is faith? Many have summarized faith to mean believing God for something that he has promised you. Others have said it is an instrument used for getting God to answer their prayers. But if the truth must be told, that is definitely not all there is to faith. That doesn't even begin to scratch the surface of the true meaning of this all important concept.

So what is faith if it does not believe God for something He has promised and it's not what you use to get God to answer your prayers? What is faith and why is it so important?

Yes, there are a thousand and one definitions of faith out there but I will like to point one of them out to you that really drives home the point for me. It is the one that says "faith is the substance of things hoped for and the evidence of things not seen."

Have you ever had hopes for something before? Have you ever felt like something that you couldn't see yet was possible for you? Have you ever looked into the future with some kind of anticipation of good associated with it? If you have, then you have hoped before.

However, something we must understand about hope is the fact that hope is always in the future tense. We only hope for things that are to come in the future and never in the present. That in itself makes hope look abstract sometimes but this is where faith comes in!

Whereas hope is to look into the future with great anticipation of good, faith is a present day assurance of that good. Faith is something you have right now that assures you of that for which you hope. Faith is today's guarantee of tomorrow's hope. Faith is the tangible part of your intangible hope.

"Faith is to believe what you do not see; the reward of this faith is to see what you believe."

- Saint Augustine

Let me illustrate the difference between faith and hope with this example. Assume that you walked into a furniture store and found a set of furniture that you really liked. You called the attention of the sales people to the furniture and asked for a particular color. For some reason, that color wasn't available in the store. Nevertheless, they assured you they could place an order for it and deliver it to your house in 2 days if you paid for it at once.

Now, look at these two likely scenarios. You either pay for it and go home to wait for the delivery or you walk out of that place hoping that you will be back for it later. If you walked out of that place without paying for the furniture but intending to come back in 2 days for it, what you walked out with is hope. You have hope that in 2 days time, you would get the furniture. On the other hand, if you paid for the furniture at once, got a receipt and walked out of the place, you don't just have hope anymore, you have faith! What's the difference?

Faith is when you have a present day proof and guarantee that what you hope for will come to pass but hope has no such guarantee. It just looks forward to the delivery of the good in the future.

The man who paid for the furniture has a receipt in his hand. He may not have walked out of the shop with the furniture but he is not different from the person who came there 5 days ago and bought the same furniture. He is as much an owner of that furniture as the man who bought his one the previous week. But the same cannot be said for the man who only has hope. At least not until the day he pays and takes delivery of his own.

Faith is what makes you an owner of something even before it is in your hands! It is what gives life to your hope.

It turns hope from being an abstract expectation to an expectation with guarantee. Whereas hopes may be dashed, faith never gets dashed! It is a firm assurance of the reality of what you hope for. It is the assurance that the result you are hoping for will not pass you by.

That is why when applied in the context of prayer; faith means that you have what you prayed for even before it id delivered to you in the physical world.

Now, lets bring it back to our theme subject.

You cannot be talking about living a self-fulfilling life without the element of faith. Just hoping for a fulfilling life is not enough. Just hoping that things will turn out right is not enough. As a matter of fact, things don't always turn out as we hope they would. It is only the force of faith that guarantees you of any real results in life.

Faith is knowing deep down inside you right now that what you desire and hope for will come to pass no matter what. It is what gives you the courage to navigate through life's curves and bend with confidence. It creates within you a kind of confidence that causes you to work and labor expecting a definite result. It makes your efforts in life worthwhile.

Did you know that there are million out there living a life of frustration because they are working and exerting themselves but aren't necessarily getting the kind of result they hope and expect for? Do you have the faintest idea how many people even end up taking their own lives out of the frustration of working like an elephant and seeing results like an ant? What they lacked in their self-fulfillment toolbox is what I call faith!

"Faith is not belief without proof, but trust without reservation."

-D. Elton Trueblood

Sometimes, life can be overwhelming. Life can seem to be moving faster than we can catch up with. There can be so much going on around our lives that we lose our sight of what matters the most. This is where faith comes in again. This is where we get to appreciate the importance of faith in the pursuit of life's purpose. Faith is the ability to look ahead and see those things that eyes cannot yet see physically.

As much as we emphasize the importance of having a vision, what most people do not understand is that every vision requires a process of time for its fulfillment. In every vision, we must all be aware that there is an interval between "the promise" and "the provision/fulfillment" of the vision. That interval is best described as "the process".

The fact that people aren't conscious of the process is the reason why many fall by the way side in their pursuit of their dreams. It is during that process that many get discouraged, give up and never attain fulfillment in their lives.

What they failed to realize is that it takes faith to follow through the required process for the fulfillment of a vision. In fact, most of what we call failure in terms of visions and dreams aren't exactly vision failures. They were always great visions with great promises but lacked the element of faith. They were powerful vision that we borne by people who had no faith at all. They were great visions that had great potentials but lacked the carrying element of faith.

"Many of life's failures are people who did not realize how close they were to success when they gave up."

- Thomas A. Edison

Faith is what it takes to stand the test of time. Faith is what it takes to wage war against the forces of distraction, discouragement and the likes. It is your faith that gives substance to the things you hope for and gives evidence to the things you do not see. It makes something that isn't yet in the natural feel so real and tangible that it becomes impossible for them not to manifest in the physical.

Faith Is The Sixth Sense

Let's face it, the world we live in right now is a physical world. Things are only considered real the moment they are manifested in the natural. No matter how great whatever your dream may be, it is never considered real until it materializes into something that can be felt, seen or heard.

Take for example, did you know that a child's birthdate on paper isn't exactly the day the child began to exist? As a matter of fact, medical science shows us that the child's heart begins to beat months before he is born into this world. But for some reason, the date that he is eventually considered a human being is the day he comes out of his mother's womb. No serious consideration is paid to all that had been going on inside the womb before that day.

Once again, this is because the world doesn't have the parameters to consider what isn't yet revealed to the natural as real. Only faith can help you relate with what may not be physically palpable as real in the now.

That is why it is so important that your faith is living and active. It is the only true connection between the dreams of your heart and the physical world. Faith helps you to carry the pregnancy of that dream all the way to term and deliver it safely into the world for all to see and benefit from. Without it, dreams are spontaneously aborted and fulfillments are forever elusive!

Life is a lot deeper than what you can see, feel, hear or relate with by using your natural senses. As a matter of fact, if all you can see is all that your eyes can see, then you are no different from the man who has no eyes.

I remember a story once told about a little girl who went on a cruise ship with her dad. As they sailed off the shores, people began to stand out on the balconies to see the beautiful sights. The girl observed that the people were excited as they looked. She tried to stretch herself to see what they were seeing but to no avail because of her height. She then became sad and began to cry. Her dad quickly asked her what the matter was and she said she couldn't see what everyone was seeing.

Immediately, daddy told her that was not a problem. He offered to carry her on his shoulders so she could see. Excited about the opportunity, she smiled and quickly raised her hand to be carried. As soon as she was on her dad shoulder, she started screaming and pointing in every direction for her dad to see what she was seeing. "Daddy look" she said. And when daddy looked he couldn't see much except for the vast expanse of sea.

She screamed repeatedly "daddy look, daddy look". Then daddy asked her what she was seeing. Guess what the little girl said? She said she "I can see farther than I can look" That day, the little girl gave one of the best descriptions of faith you can ever have. It is the ability to see farther than you can look and to act correspondingly!

If you want to know what self-fulfillment truly is, you need inside information. You need to see something that others don't see and be motivated by that higher vision that you have. It is faith that helps you capture a vision bigger and greater than your imagination or explanation. Actually, we can safely say that the measure of fulfillment you will enjoy in your life will be directly proportional to how you walk by faith.

In other to attain self-fulfillment in life, you have got to be different from the masses. You have to stand out from the rest of the world who cant see beyond their nose. It is that extra sense with which you perceive deeper realities that separates you from the rest. Now, guess what? Faith is that extra sense that help you to see what ordinary eyes don't see and hear what ordinary ears don't hear. Faith gives you access to superior information that literally gives you the advantage in life.

By faith you can make contact with realities that are not yet revealed to the human senses. That way, you will always be miles ahead of the rest of the world.

Faith opens your mind to a whole new world of possibility that could otherwise not be seen. In fact, those who ever did any mighty work in ancient times were described to have done that by the use of their faith.

Faith Is An Action Stimulant, It Believes And Then Acts

If there is anything that leads to true success and accomplishment in this world, it is the ability to take the right actions at the right times. Success is always the result of action rather than mere wishes. But many times, people are so timid they can't even list a finger. You see, one thing I love about faith is that it is not just the ability to see into the future, it is the ability to step out into fulfilling it.

No matter how great a future you see and hope for, until you take steps towards its fulfillment, it will only remain something you hope for or a dream you cherish in your heart. It is the action you take towards it fulfillment that hastens its fulfillment.

The amazing story of Charles Blondin, a famous French tightrope walker, is a wonderful illustration of what true faith is.

Blondin's greatest fame came on September 14, 1860, when he became the first person to cross a tightrope stretched 11,000 feet (over a quarter of a mile) across the mighty Niagara Falls. People from both Canada and America came from miles away to see this great feat.

He walked across, 160 feet above the falls, several times... each time with a different daring feat - once in a sack, on stilts, on a bicycle, in the dark, and blindfolded. One time he even carried a stove and cooked an omelet in the middle of the rope!

A large crowd gathered and the buzz of excitement ran along both sides of the river bank. The crowd "Oohed and Aahed!" as Blondin carefully walked across - one dangerous step after another - pushing a wheelbarrow holding a sack of potatoes.

Then at one point, he asked for the participation of a volunteer. Upon reaching the other side, the crowd's applause was louder than the roar of the falls!

Blondin suddenly stopped and addressed his audience: «Do you believe I can carry a person across in this wheelbarrow?»

The crowd enthusiastically yelled, «Yes! You are the greatest tightrope walker in the world. We believe!»

«Okay,» said Blondin, «Who wants to get into the wheelbarrow.»

As far as the Blondin's story goes, no one did at the time!

This unique story illustrates a real life picture of what faith actually is. The crowd watched these daring feats. They said they believed. But... their actions proved they truly did not believe. Faith never says it believes and then becomes reluctant to act out the believing. Faith always acts in line with its belief and convictions.

It is one thing for us to say we believe in the future and al that. It's one thing for us to say we believe in the reality of a life of fulfillment but then, it's a completely different thing to demonstrate real faith.

Hundred Reasons To Smile

When the winds of life blow and all hope seems lost, faith gives you a reason to smile and hope again. When life hits you below the belt and all you feel like doing is to give it all up, faith gives you that assurance of a better life and future. How then can anyone imagine that he can live a fulfilling life without it? That is practically impossible my friend.

A blind boy sat on the steps of a building with a hat by his feet. He had a sign which read: «I am blind. Please Help.» There were only a few coins in the hat.

When a man came walking by, he took a few coins from his pocket and dropped them into the hat. Then he took the sign, turned it around, and wrote some words on the back. He put the sign where it was, so that everyone who walked by would see the new words.

Soon the hat began to fill up. A lot more people were giving money to the blind boy.

That afternoon the man who had changed the sign came to see how things were going. The boy recognized his footsteps and asked, «Were you the one who changed my sign this morning? What did you write?»

The man said, «I only wrote the truth. I said what you said but in a different way. I wrote: 'Today is a beautiful day, but I cannot see it.'»

Both signs told people the same thing... that the boy was blind. But the first sign simply said the boy was blind. The second sign told people they were extremely fortunate that they were not blind. Should we be surprised that the second sign was more effective?

Be thankful for what you have. Be creative. Be innovative. Think differently and positively.

When life gives you a reason to cry, show life that you have 100 reasons to smile. Face your past without regret. Handle your present with confidence. Prepare for the future without fear.

Keep the faith and drop the fear... just remember God is near!

You see, no matter how bad things get, somehow; faith always sees the good in every situation. It sees the possibilities where we think there is none. It see answers even in the midst of the most difficult questions of life.

"The keys to patience are acceptance and faith. Accept things as they are, and look realistically at the world around you. Have faith in yourself and in the direction you have chosen."

- Ralph Marston

Another perfect example here is the story of Abraham who was 75 years old and had no child. Naturally speaking, he should forget about having children in his lifetime. He should just resign to fate and leave that dream for others who still have nature on their side. To make matters worse, his wife Sarah was 65 years old!

If you have any knowledge of biology and how the human reproductive organs function, you would agree that having kids was far away from being possible for this couple. But then, God told the same Abraham that he was going to become the father of many nations. It has to be a matter of faith for anyone to believe such a statement. The person has to see something beyond the natural realm. The person has to see something more than what biology and reproductive systems show. And that was exactly what they did.

Their faith in this case was hinged on God who made the promise and His ability to deliver. The only reason they could dare to believe was because it was God who said so. This is what I call the God-Dimension of faith. This is the type of faith that is based on what God has said concerning you and the future. You hold on to that no matter what evidences appear in the natural.

There may be a thousand and one reason why your dreams would not come through. There may be several factors against the fulfillment of your purpose in life. But with faith, you can trust and hope for the best. You can bet your life on the fact that your dreams will still come through no matter what.

Let me tell you something that might be little shocking to you. Believing in the fulfillment of your dreams and aspirations alone is not enough to bring you fulfillment in life. Until you believe enough to act on what you believe, I dare say you aren't yet a believer my dear friend. Until you believe in such a way that it moves you into a correspondent action, you haven't truly believed.

"Faith is taking the first step even when you don't see the whole staircase."

- Martin Luther King, Jr.

Fulfillment in life is like a whole staircase. Whereas, faith helps you to see the top of the staircase, it is the actions that you take that helps you ascent up the staircase. You have to understand that the fact that you can see the top of the stairs will never get you there so you must act.

Faith Always Knows Where It's Going!

In January 2000, leaders in Charlotte , North Carolina, invited their favorite son, Billy Graham, to a luncheon in his honor.

Billy initially hesitated to accept the invitation because he struggled with Parkinson's disease. But the Charlotte leaders said, «We don't expect a major address. Just come and let us honor you.» So he agreed.

After wonderful things were said about him, Dr. Graham stepped to the rostrum, looked at the crowd, and said, «I'm reminded today of Albert Einstein, the great physicist who this month has been honored by Time Magazine as the 'Man of the Century'.

Einstein was once traveling from Princeton on a train when the conductor came down the aisle, punching the tickets of every passenger. When he came to Einstein, Einstein reached in his vest pocket. He couldn't find his ticket, so he reached in his trouser pockets. It wasn't there, so he looked in his briefcase but couldn't find it. Then he looked in the seat beside him. He still couldn't find it.

The conductor said, 'Dr. Einstein, I know who you are. We all know who you are. I'm sure you bought a ticket. Don't worry about it.'

Einstein nodded appreciatively. The conductor continued down the aisle punching tickets. As he was ready to move to the next car, he turned around and saw the great physicist down on his hands and knees looking under his seat for his ticket.

The conductor rushed back and said, 'Dr. Einstein, Dr. Einstein, don't worry, I know who you are No problem. You don't need a ticket. I'm sure you bought one.'

Einstein looked at him and said, 'Young man, I too, know who I am. What I don't know is where I'm going.'»

"Faith is a knowledge within the heart, beyond the reach of proof."

-Khalil Gibran

Faith isn't that way. No matter how dark life gets, faith always knows where it is going. It always has its eyes fixed on where it is going. Little wonder why some other sources rightly defined faith as

"… The firm foundation under everything that makes life worth living. It's our handle on what we can't see."

Chapter 11

You Must Discover Your Calling

Chapter 11
You Must Discover Your Calling

Who among us could live without computers today? It seems they are everywhere – in our studies at home, on our desks at work, in the library, the bank and even the cafe. We get pleasure from them, we swear at them, we need them.

But it's only a recent thing. Just 3 generations ago the Chairman of IBM declared there is a world market for only five computers. As recently as 1977 the President of Digital Equipment claimed there is no reason anyone would want a computer in their home!

The revolution was brought to us in large part by Steven Jobs, the founder of Apple Computers. Steve Jobs was just 21 when he and Steve Wozniak invented the Apple Computer. Until then computers were a monstrous mass of vacuum tubes which took whole rooms. Then the two Steve's managed to take that mass of tubes and incorporate them inside a box small enough to sit on a desk.

Jobs and Wozniak offered their invention to Atari. They weren't interested in big bucks – all they wanted was a salary and the opportunity to continue their work. Atari knocked them back. They offered it to Hewlett-Packard, but Hewlett Packard knocked them back. It seemed Jobs and Wozniak alone could see the possibilities. So Jobs sold his Volkswagon and Wozniak sold his calculator, and with the $1300 that gave them they formed Apple Computers. The company was named Apple in memory of a happy summer Jobs had spent working in an orchard.

The rest is history. By all accounts Steve Jobs is a visionary, and spurred on by that vision he built a successful computer company. But Jobs soon discovered that if his vision was to reach fruition they needed greater management expertise. So Jobs approached John Sculley, then President of PepsiCo. There was absolutely no reason why Sculley should leave a highly paid position in a world leading company to go work with a bunch of computer nerds in a fledgling industry.

Not unsurprisingly he turned Jobs down. But Jobs wouldn't take no for an answer. He approached Sculley again. Again Sculley turned him down. In a last ditch effort Jobs passionately presented his visionary ideas to Sculley and he asked Sculley a question that forced him to accept. The question was this:

"Do you want to spend the rest of your life selling sugared water or do you want a chance to change the world?"

- Steve Jobs

Let me ask you a similar question right now. Do you want to spend the rest of your life just doing a job or do you want a chance to change the world?

If the later is your answer like I expect, then you have to discover your calling. You have to find out what you are here for and go all out in pursuit of it. In reality my dear, it is only those who have found out their unique place in the world that really get that chance to change the world. It is only those who set out to fulfill their unique calling that come to realize what true fulfillment in life is.

«The whole secret of a successful life is to find out what is one's destiny to do, and then do it.»

- Henry Ford

I dare say that until you find out what you are destined to do, you are merely existing but not living yet. Until you can confidently say, "the reason I am alive is to …" you are really not going to know what fulfillment is in this world. As a matter of fact, a life of fulfillment and satisfaction really begins only after the discovery of its purpose. I have a different book where I show you how to discover you purpose in life but in this chapter, I am going to point you towards the steps to take in other to discover the very reason for your existence. Then I will even show you practical tips to take in other to maximally fulfill that purpose.

No Fulfillment Outside Your Calling

That ultimate reason for which you were born is what is referred to as your calling. The reason why your birth became necessary in the first place is your calling. Until you discover it and pursue it, it is going to be impossible to live a fulfilled life here on earth. In fact, this is where fulfillment becomes different from just success.

Whereas success is the achievement of an aim or purpose, fulfillment comes from the achievement of your destined purpose and assignment. In other words, it is one thing for you to get involved with anything you choose and through the application of the principles of success turn out successful in it. But it is a totally different ball game to turn our successful in what your life was given for in the first place.

When you succeed at just anything, it is just another achievement to your credit but when you succeed at fulfilling your calling then that is true fulfillment there.

«Our greatest fear should not be of failure... but of succeeding at things in life that don't really matter.»

- Francis Chan

How important it is to understand this concept. Imagine the number of people out there chasing shadows in hope that it might lead them to fulfillment in life. Imagine the myriads of people out there who might appear to others to be successful but in the true sense of it, they are only but glorified failures! Somewhere deep down inside them, they are the most miserable people alive.

Specifically, I remember the story of a certain rich man who had worked all his life to acquire the good things of life. But for reason then unknown to him, the more of the goodies of life he acquired, the more empty he felt about life. He tried some more in hopes that by the time he has attained a higher height, he would become satisfied with life.

However, that was not to be. The harder he tried, the more empty he felt until one day he couldn't take it no more. He went down to the bank of a river and determined to drown to death. He went at a time of the day when there would be no one around to save him because he really wanted to end it all. He was tired of the misery he was living in. he was tired of living a life where others think he was successful and well off but deep inside him, there was this void longing to be filled.

After looking around and finding no one, he dived right into the body of water. Unknown to him, another man had come there to think about his life too and was sitting somewhere not too far away. The man saw this rich man struggling inside the water and quickly came to his rescue. When they got on land and he was resuscitated, he looked at his savior who was expecting to hear a hearty thank you and said "why did you save me?" and began to cry!

For a moment, the savior was confused. He didn't know what to think anymore. Here he was risking his own life to save someone from drowning and all he gets is "why did you save me?" He then asked the rich man "why did you want to kill yourself?" That was when the rich man began to narrate how hard he had worked for the things he had achieved in his life but how empty he still felt. He explained that with all his accomplishments, there is still a big void in his life that wouldn't close up. He explained that it appears like with every new achievement to his credit, the void even gets bigger. It was when he could no longer take it that he decided to end his own life.

You see my friend, there is nothing wrong with being rich. There is nothing wrong with being successful. There is nothing wrong with achieving and accomplishing big things only as long as those achievements are in line with your calling. It is only when you walk in line with your calling that you are assured of a life of fulfillment. That is when you are assured of a life without that emptiness and void the rich man and several others experience even today.

«I believe every human has a finite number of heartbeats.
I don't intend to waste any of mine.»

- Neil Armstrong

You have just one life to live so don't waste it. Don't live your life running a lost race. There are rules in every game and so is it with life itself. There are rules for living a fulfilling life and a paramount one is for you to live it in pursuit of your calling and purpose.

Take for instance, in a running completion; the winner isn't just going to be the guy who gets to the finish line first. The winner is always the one who gets to the finish line without breaking any of the rules of the game. It takes both speed and playing by the rules to get the gold medal.

For example, as a rule; athletes should never cross over to another lane as they race towards the finish line. If for any reason they do, they will be disqualified from the race. So it doesn't matter that the guy was the first to get to the finish line, as long as he crossed out of his lane, he is disqualified from getting the medal.

Interestingly, it's the same thing with life for us. It is not about getting to the finishing line first. It's not about beating everyone to it. It's about ensuring that you stayed in tune with your own lane in life. It's about ensuring that you ran your race in a way that led to the fulfillment of the reason for your life. Always bear in mind that in life, it's not always the person who has achieved the most that is crowned. It is the one who has achieved the most of what he was sent to achieve. So don't live your life running on a wrong track. Don't live your life running another man's race or chasing after the wrong things.

Like that rich man, you might have had your own fair share of a life full of so much void that only walking in your calling can satisfy. You may have labored to attain every height imaginable only to discover that all that doesn't amount to much. Don't worry though, you are discovering the missing part of that puzzle right now.

Maybe, yours has been a life full of endless pursuits. You have always believed that when you achieve this or achieve that, you will be fine. Then let me save you the agony before it's too late. There is no true fulfillment in things. There is even no fulfillment in mere achievements and accomplishments. It is only walking in your calling that leads to true fulfillment in life.

According to the dictionary, fulfillment is the achievement of something predicted. It is not just the achievement of anything but the achievement of that which has been predicted. Your calling is the prediction of what you are supposed to do in life. It is the prediction of what you were born to achieve. Therefore, it is only when you step out to accomplish that which has been predicted for you that you really have that amazing feeling of fulfillment.

«The two most important days in your life are the day you are born and the day you find out why.»

- Mark Twain

Yes, you have been born already but have you found out why? Have you discovered why you were born or you are busy chasing after your own agenda? You must realize that you cant find fulfillment in life by chasing after shadows. You cant find satisfaction by chasing after your own agenda.

Whether you knew it or not, there was an agenda for which your birth became necessary and it is only in the pursuit of that agenda that you can find the joy of living.

We can all engage ourselves in various occupations and professions. We can do whatsoever we decide or desire to do but then, true fulfillment only comes when we do what we were created to do. You are not here for nothing. You were not placed here to find a job. You weren't even placed here to make a living. You are only here because there is a need in your generation that the solution has been placed in you. Until you set out to do that, you will only be going round and round in circles. Until you set out to do that, you really wont find the fulfilment you are looking for.

Stop Living To Make Money

Anybody can get a job, but sadly, just getting a job doesn't begin to equate to living a fulfilled life. There are million and millions of people out there with good paying jobs that aren't fulfilled. There are millions of people out there with great jobs but still feel like something is missing in their lives because what it take to live a meaningful life is not a good job.

Therefore, stop thinking that if only you got a job everything will be alright. I am sorry to burst your bubbles but that doesn't guarantee that everything will be fine. It is walking in your calling that guarantees everything will be fine. More than getting a job, what is important is for you to fulfill destiny.

«I don't want to get to the end of my life and find that I lived just the length of it. I want to have lived the width of it as well.»

– Diane Ackerman

Oh how thoughtful this is! Maybe you haven't really given it a thought yourself but I guess you can do that now. Do you really want to get to the end of life and then discover that all that you have to show for the life you lived was just the length of it? Do you want to live a life that is only measured in the years that you lived or one that is measured is the depth of impact and difference that you made? Like someone rightly said, you don't have to change the whole world to make a difference, you only have to change someone's world.

You were created specifically to change someone's world. You were put here on earth for a particular assignment. And according to the design of the maker, it is only in that place of assignment that you can get to experience real fulfillment and satisfaction in life. Whatever you do, please discover your purpose. Whatever you do, wherever you go, please make sure to discover that particular assignment you were created for and go after it with all your heart.

By the way, I have discovered that many times when we tell people to go after their purpose and do what they were born to do, a question that arises is the fact that they need to make money. They consider that if they go after their purpose and passion, they will not be able to pay their bills so they stay with what they call job security!

Listen dear, no job can offer you any form of security if you are not working in line with your calling. No job can offer you any stability if it is away from your purpose. As a matter of fact, what you will be doing by taking on that job is what I like to refer to as mortgaging the future because the time you should have spent pursuing purpose was spent chasing after money.

Let me tell you one secret right now. If you truly discover your purpose and go after it with all your heart and might, money will come as a byproduct.

How Do You Discover Your Calling?

Sheryl was in the middle of a successful career as an electrical engineer. She was paid well, had been promoted twice, and was now beginning to manage projects—but she was miserable. For one thing, her recent move to project manager had not gone smoothly. She clashed with coworkers and felt little control or support when problems came up that needed solving. It was stressful. For another thing, the project manager role gave her a reason to take a step back and look at the big picture of what she was doing with her work.

Her company specialized in developing innovative, high-end speaker systems, and the work rang hollow to her. "In the grand scheme of things, I just don't feel like what I'm doing is really making a difference. I want to wake up in the morning eager to go to work, spend the day excited about what I'm doing, and at the end of the day I want to look at myself in the mirror and feel like what I did that day mattered. I have never thought of my work as a calling, but that's exactly what I long for. How can I find it?"

Sheryl began with an informal assessment of her gifts and also took a battery of tests. Her interest profile suggested that she enjoyed mechanical and intellectual tasks, especially those that provided an outlet for creative self-expression. Her personality scores suggested that she was extremely conscientious, open to experience, and neurotic; she had an average level of agreeableness and was not very extroverted.

Her profile of abilities suggested that she was adept at reasoning with numbers and accurately understanding and mentally manipulating spatial patterns. She mentioned that she could write well, which was consistent with a very high verbal-ability score. Her values suggested that it was most important for her to have a feeling of accomplishment on the job, to have a chance to try out her own ideas, to have support from her supervisors, and to feel like her work benefited others.

The mismatch between her gifts and what she was doing in her current job started to become clear for Sheryl. Engineering fit well for her as a profession—indeed, she loved her current job when she first started—but the project manager role didn't feel right from the start. She had to give up some of the hands-on work she loved to focus on the tasks of managing people (which, she quickly found out, she didn't love); hence, her interests were not well satisfied.

Her high neuroticism meant she was highly vulnerable to job-related stress (of which she had a lot), and her low extraversion did not make it any easier to manage people the way she felt she must. Her abilities were partially satisfied: she could map out well what needed to be done, and her written reports were outstanding, but when challenges arose or her coworkers' performance wasn't up to par, relationships quickly became strained and she felt overwhelmed and unable to handle it. Her values? In theory she should have felt like she was accomplishing things, but because her team members were doing the nuts and bolts of the projects, she felt a step removed from the work itself.

Her ideas were sometimes challenged by know-it-all coworkers, and although she felt supported when she was a subordinate, as a project manager she felt more or less on her own.

Questions followed. What now? Should she ask her company to move her back into a staff engineer role, possibly closing herself off from future promotions? Should she try to obtain some training and support to make the manager role work? Or should she consider starting over at another company? Maybe her current misery was telling her that another occupation altogether might be a better fit—something in medical science, for example, or technical writing, two possibilities that her test results suggested, along with engineering.

Here we run into the limits of processing the parameters of personal fit, of looking only at the role of actor as a level of analysis. Sheryl said she longed for a sense of calling. What is her work all about, in an ultimate sense? How does her work fit in the broader context of her life, and with her broader sense of purpose? How does it contribute to the world around her? What kinds of needs in the world matter to her and beckon for her attention? Such questions require a more expansive approach to looking at the problem.

I have found that just like Sheryl, many people make it look mysterious to discover thier purpose when it is not. They try to over spiritualize and over analyze something that is so clear and in the open. In fact, your calling is written all over you right now. Your calling is so glaring that only if you looked in the right direction you would very easily pick it up.

You have to understand that everything about you and your life was custom designed in line with the purpose for which you were created. Every single feature that makes you up was put there to support the reason why you were placed here. For example, when a car manufacturer is designing a car, no matter how beautiful they design the body, they know that the car will not move without an engine inside to propel it. Therefore, they endeavor to add an engine into the build and makeup of the car. It doesn't matter whether it is placed in front or at the back, there just has to be an engine in that car for it to move around. For the same reason, they add tires to the vehicle to ensure smooth functioning according to its purpose.

In the same way, when the manufacturer of a smart phone is about to create a smart phone, he also has to decide on how he wants the phone to function. If he wants a touch sensitive phone, he adds a touch screen feature there. But if the phone is designed to function by key pads, there will be no need for a touch sensitive screen.

In both the case of the car and the phone, the best way to know the purpose and calling of these things is to look at what was put in them by the manufacturer. The appearance of tire tells us that this thing is supposed to move and not stand like a statue in the garage. The absence of a keypad tells us that the screen should be touch sensitive in the case of the phone.

In the same way, God has put certain things in you to help you discover and identify your purpose and calling. I have a whole book on this titled "Who Am I" but for the purpose of this topic, I will like to point out 5 ways to discover your purpose now.

"I believe there's a calling for all of us. I know that every human being has value and purpose. The real work of our lives is to become aware. And awakened. To answer the call."

\- Oprah Winfrey

1. Your Purpose Is In Your Desires:

Let me tell you a secret right now my dear. Everyone doesn't desire the same things as you do! Your desires and interest are as unique to you as your calling and purpose is. So to find out your purpose, lets find out what your desires are. What thrills you and what makes you tick?

What is that desire you have that has refused to go over the years? What is that desire that you have that just refuses to be satisfied. The more you fulfill the desire, the more you desire it. That is a clear indication of what you are called to do my friend.

2. Your Purpose Is In Your Passion:

Your passion is another clear indication of what you are called to do. By passion, we are talking about something you love and enjoy doing. Something that comes natural to you. More like a hobby but with a stronger desire that just a hobby.

Your passion is something you enjoy so much you forget about time when you do it. You forget about food and everything else when it comes to this thing. In fact, you can trade the whole world just to do this particular thing. It is literally all that matters to you in life. It is that thing you will do over and over again even if no one ever paid you for it. As far as you are concerned, the satisfaction of doing it far outweighs any amount anyone could possible give you.

If you haven't found your passion, then find it because your passion will always lead you to your purpose and calling.

3. Your Purpose Is In Your Hatred:

Now, lets look at the near opposite of what I just talked about. Whether we like it or not, we all have some form if hatred and dissatisfaction with one thing or the other in life. It might be a certain problem of the world that you have so much. It might be a certain need among a certain group of people that gets to you this much. Whatever it is, find out what you hate.

Life has a way of creating a special hatred for the problem or circumstance you were born to solve. Having considered your desires and passion, also consider your hatred. That thing you hate with a passion might just be what you were born to solve. You have no idea how many people living in this word are already suffering from it now. You have to rise up to the challenge and become the deliverer and savior in your sphere of influence.

4. Your Purpose Is In Your Gifts & Talents:

A gift or talent is a natural ability or skill that you have. It is something you can do very well even though you didn't learn how to do it. It is something you were born into this world with. Now, let me ask you. Why will God put a gift or talent in you if it has nothing to do with why you were born?

Just as the case of the manufacturer I talked about, there is no way under heave that God would have put stuffs in you that weren't meant to enhance your calling. So look at your gifts, look at your talents. What can you do with them? Where can it be useful? How can it help change the world?

You may not exactly now your definite calling but I guarantee you that following your gifts and talents is one sure way that will lead you to it.

Your Purpose Is In Your Ideas: Books have been written and course have been taught on the power of the mind and how we should use it. Yet many haven't discovered how connected the working of their mind is to their purpose and calling in life. If you take a close look at your life, you will discover that you are kind of inclined to getting ideas in a certain direction. There seems to be a certain area of life where you are always having ideas and dreams of what should be done that isn't done yet. Now let me tell you another secret.

It is impossible for you to receive an idea that you cannot make happen. It is impossible for you to receive a dream that cannot be fulfilled. Actually, the mere fact that you got that idea means that you have what it takes to bring it to fruition. So why don't you begin by bringing those consistent and recurrent ideas to pass? That's a good way to begin to understand and experience self-fulfillment in life I tell you.

5. Most Importantly, Ask God!

"You were created in the image of God. And it is only through God that you can find the true meaning of life. And it is only through God that you can truly find fulfillment. And it is only through God's Son, the Lord Jesus Christ, that you can be saved."

- Calvin W. Allison

No one ever knows the purpose or use of a product better than the manufacturer. Therefore, the best person to ask when in doubt about the purpose of a thing is the one who made it.

Yes, you can find your calling and purpose by following all those clues and leadings I have described above, but you will agree with me that nothing serves better than asking God – the manufacturer.

Don't Waste Your Life

"There is no passion to be found playing small, in settling for a life that is less than the one you are capable of living"

– Nelson Mandela

Knowing that you only get to live once, I will totally agree with Nelson Mandela that it is no use playing small. It is no use settling for a life that is less than the one you are capable of living. It is no use living a life that doesn't fulfill the purpose for which it was given.

You see, when your life goal is known, you don't waste time wandering about life. When your life's goal is known, you don't join the bunch of people who are just beating around the bush and going through the motion in their lives. Rather you face life head on and give a knock out!

People that are sure of their callings become fulfilled faster in life. People that discover their callings will more easily achieve greatness than those who don't know where they are going. The discovery of your purpose will accelerate your fulfillment in life so go ahead and find out yours now if you haven't done so already.

Chapter 12

Your Dream Is A Myth Without Work

Chapter 12
Your Dream Is A Myth Without Work

We all have them. High hopes, wishes, dreams, expectations for the days ahead, call it any name you wish. From parents who hope that their children will succeed than themselves in life to youths who hope for a better life than they were ever accustomed to. To college students who dream of life after college and the opportunities that will accrue to them on the basis of their degrees.

Even business men who are optimistic about a flourishing business year as they carefully forecast what their revenue would be are not left out. The truth is that virtually everyone in every sector and every sphere of human endeavor have dreams. As a matter of fact, we will be right to say that the problem in the world is not that of lack of dreamers. It's not even the fact that there are no people with vision.

However, the major problems facing our world today is the fact that many have been brainwashed into believing that dreams and visions are all they need to live a fulfilled life. Oh far too many people have been lied to that once they have a dream their life will become a plethora of happiness and fulfillment. Not knowing better, these people keep their dreams alive for a year, two, five, ten years and in some cases even more. But at the end, all they get are unrealized dreams that have metamorphosed into objects of depression and frustration.

What used to be a dream and hope for a better future now turns to a source of unworthiness. Sadly, when people find themselves at this bridge, they have no clue on how to cross it. They simply do not know how to convert their dreams and wishes into a tangible reality. However, I must have you know that what has kept your dreams as mere wishes all along is the fact that you never took commensurate actions to realize them.

Friends, it is what we do with our dreams that makes us get the results we hope for. The corresponding steps and actions that we take when we have all these wonderful ideas and dreams is what brings us fulfillment in life.

Take for example, a child that is used to dreaming and fantasizing about becoming a doctor. Let's say he gets so engrossed in that fantasy that every night he sleeps, he finds himself in the theatre performing surgeries. Now let's think about it together, for how long does he need to keep that dream alive to become a doctor without going to a medical school? Yeah, your guess is as good as mine… Donkey years!

The truth is that it does not matter how many times he dreams of being a doctor at night or how strong his desire for the profession of medicine is; until he gets up and does all it takes to get admitted into a medical school, it will only be a dream. One that will never be realized for that matter. Mind you, the reason it will never be realized has nothing to do with the whether the dream is right or wrong for him in life. It's just the consequence of his refusal to take the necessary actions to bring that dream to pass.

Listen, for every dream conceived in this world, there is a required action. For every dream that enters the heart of a man, there are things that must be done if the dream will ever be fulfilled. This is what many have been missing in their lives and I don't want you to miss it too.

Why do you think the book of Acts in the bible was so called? Is it because it gives an account of people with great dreams. Oh no! Absolutely not. Rather it is so called because that is exactly what it is. It is actually a compilation of the actions of men and women who walked this earth we are walking today; many years ago. It is a documentation of what our predecessors did and not what they dreamt of doing.

Careful observation shows that there was no dream recorded in there. Why then do you want to reverse the order in your life? Why do you want to remain a dreamer with no actions? For you to live fulfilled you must be an actor not just a dreamer and you must always be proactive.

Really nothing happens of serious consequence on earth without hard work.

"There can be no richer man or woman than the individual who has found his or her labor of love. Personal fulfillment through the virtue of work is the highest form of desire. Work is the conduit between the supply and the demand of all human needs, the forerunner of human progress, and the medium by which the imagination is given the wings of action. A labor of love is exalted because it provides joy and self-expression to those who perform it"

– Dennis Kimbro

When Jesus saw the enormous harvest of souls, He didn't ask for preachers and evangelists. He asked for laborers. It doesn't matter what your title is, what matters is your ability to work hard. Hard work is the wealth of the poor man. If you can work hard, you are a wealthy man. It is this wealth of hard work that converts everything else into cash and currency.

Work Removes All The Cares Of The World

Let me share with you the story of a fisherman I heard some time ago.

One day a fisherman was lying on a beautiful beach with his fishing pole propped up in the sand and his solitary line cast out into the sparkling blue surf. He was enjoying the warmth of the afternoon sun and the prospect of catching a fish or two.

At about that time, a salesman came strolling along the beach in a bid to relieve some of the stress of his workday. He noticed the fisherman sitting on the beach nonchalantly and decided to find out why this fisherman was just lazing away at the peak of work hours instead of working harder to make a living for himself and his family.

«You aren't going to catch many fishes that way,» said the salesman to the fisherman, and he went further to lecture him saying «you should be working rather than lying on the beach!»

The fisherman looked up at the salesman, smiled and replied, «And what will my reward be for working harder?»

«Well, you can get bigger nets and catch more fishes!» responded the salesman eagerly.

«So, if I get bigger nets and catch more fishes, what
will my reward be?»
asked the fisherman again, still smiling.

The salesman replied,
«Of course you will make money and you'll be able to buy a
boat which will then result in larger catches of fish!»

«And yet again what will my reward be for having a larger
boat that can catch more fishes?»
asked the fisherman.

At this point, the salesman was beginning to get exasperated
with the fisherman's questions and he replied him briskly
saying
«You can buy a bigger boat and hire some people to work
for you!»
he said.

«And then what will my reward be for working so hard,
buying a bigger boat and hiring people to work for me?»
repeated the fisherman.

Clearly the businessman was getting seriously angry and
he replied «Don't you understand? You can build up a fleet
of fishing boats, sail all over the world, and let all your
employees catch fish for you!»

Once again, calmly, the fisherman asked,
«And then what will my reward be if I put in the work to
achieve all of these things that you have mentioned?»

The businessman was livid with rage at this time and
shouted at the fisherman,
«Don't you understand that you can become so rich that
you will never have to work for your living again! You can
spend all the rest of your days sitting on this beach looking
at the sunset. You won't have a care in the world!»

The fisherman, still smiling, simply looked up, nodded and
said to the man:
«And what exactly do you think I am doing now?»
He then looked at the sunset, threw the pole he had in his
hands into the water, and laid on the beach without a care
in the world.

He had put in all the work the salesman was advocating for him to put in and was already at the point where he was enjoying the fruits of his labor!

"The price of success is hard work, dedication to the job at hand, and the determination that whether we win or lose, we have applied the best of ourselves to the task at hand."

- Vince Lombardi

Oh have you been dreaming of attaining success in life? Does your heart yearn for fulfillment? Let me tell you the hard truth. The only way to realize them is through the vehicle of hard work. I mean tireless, laborious and conscientious work. You must find a work that your heart is in and that you are passionate about and commit your entire being into it.

I once read an interview granted by Bill Gates. Of the several questions he was asked, one of them was about bequeathing his wealth to his children. Though he didn't exactly reveal what percentage of his wealth was going to his children, he stated that he already told his children that they must find a work that they love and then they must go on to do that work.

Clearly we can tell that he was just revealing the same principles that had brought him this far in life. Some ignorant fellows try to make a mockery of the fact that he was a school dropout but they often forget to tell the other half of the story that he actually dropped out to pursue the work that he loved and enjoyed.

«Your work is going to fill a large part of your life, and the only way to be truly satisfied is to do what you believe is great work. And the only way to do great work is to love what you do. If you haven't found it yet, keep looking. Don't settle. As with all matters of the heart, you'll know when you find it.»

- Steve Jobs

Friend, I would have you know that consistent hard work is the route to true fulfillment in life. Every other thing like meditating or confessing mantras will not fetch you the success and fulfillment that your heart desires. Yes, they have their place but definitely not as exaggerated as they make it seem. Yes, positive thinking is a great way to program your mind for the success you desire but it is not an end in itself.

Imagine a football team who only think and convince themselves that they have what it takes to win their next match but never shows up on the field of play. Where do you think their positivity will land them? Your guess is as good as mine!

Hard work makes you enjoy the law of sowing and reaping. The efforts, energy, time, labor and everything you put into your pursuits in life today will eventually pay off and translate into wealth for you tomorrow. When you make hard work your watch word, it may take a while but success and fulfilment will certainly be yours.

Over-night Success!

That brings me to another angle on the subject of work. And that is the concept of overnight success. Unfortunately, in these days and times, many do not appreciate the dignity of labor again. Many youths are out there whose dream is to "hit it big" and become successful overnight without any input of time or energy into any venture. Oh, they just want to sleep and wake up and receive alerts that money had been transferred into their accounts just like that. They want to afford a life of luxury and satisfaction so fast that they don't even want to give any time to work for it.

Wake up buddy, there is no such thing as reward without labor. There is no such thing as overnight success either. The world we live in is such that operates by laws and principles. When you sow in effort, time, energy with some other necessary key factor, only then are you worthy to reap the reward of wealth. Don't be deceived by people who preach the gospel of overnight success. There is nobody who is an overnight success.

All the stories they preach to you about people becoming big overnight are all embellished stories that contain half-truths. What they fail to reveal to you is that these overnight successes are people who have been at the background for 5, 6 sometimes 12 years slaving away, putting in their efforts, time, sweat, resources into the causes they believed in. It is only when the proceeds of work begin to manifest that everybody starts oohing and aahing about their projects but the truth is that they have been at it for donkey years.

As a matter of fact, Eddie Cantor – the American comedian says it takes 20 years to become an overnight success and this is the home truth. Don't let anyone pull a wool over your eyes about overnight success, it is all tales by moonlight. Roll up your sleeves, get down to work and put in your very best into pursuing your dreams, goals, passions and your assignment on earth, it will only be a matter of time before success comes calling on you.

John Daymond is an America's fashion legend who by dint of hard work shot up the ladder of success in life. He grew up in a lower middle class area of New York City, Hollis Queens. His parents got divorced and his father deserted them when he was 10 years old. Daymond never knew that, that was the last he would see or hear from him.

After his dad's exit, himself and mum became very poor and he literally became the man of the house overnight!

As the story goes, Daymond started working from the age of six. He was doing every kind of job ranging from handing out flyers in his neighborhood to selling customized pencils with student's names painted on it in school to shoveling snow in the winter and raking leaves in the fall. By the time he was 10, he had become an apprentice electrician who was already wiring PX cable in abandoned buildings in the Bronx area.

In Daymond's own words, while growing up, all of a sudden there was this amazing music. It's like what we call today a "disruptive technology." It came out of the Bronx and it made its way into Queens. It was called Hip-Hop. This music was today's Twitter. It was a way the kids were communicating about their hopes and their dreams and the plight of the community. And this music not only came with a way to talk, it came with a way to walk and a way to dress and it was engaging and I wanted to be a part of it.

There was this guy in Queens and he was becoming really well known and he was making a living selling this music and I didn't realize that you could make a living doing something you love. It was Russell Simmons and he was driving around Queens and he would put on his brother and two friends, Run DMC, then he'd find this handsome guy who liked to lick his lips a lot and wear Kangol hats named LL Cool J. Russell was all about pushing this culture and I wanted to be part of it and I didn't really know how to be part of it.

I started to want to become a part of this culture and we started wearing these clothes and we started hearing that these designers didn't want us wearing their stuff.

One company called Timberland, they're not owned by the same owners now, but they said "we don't sell our boots to drug dealers." I wasn't a drug dealer. I was a hard working young man who was working at Red Lobster as a waiter. I didn't have enough money to go to college so I had to get a job as a waiter and I was upset.

The discrimination meted out to Daymond and his friends made them team up to start their own clothing line that would be all-inclusive. They wanted a clothing line that just about anybody irrespective of their skin color can wear thus the company FUBU "For Us By Us" was born.

Daymond's mother was a good Seamstress who taught him how to sow. Once he learnt how to sow, he went to buy some cheap fabric, sewed 80 of them in his mom's living room and hit the streets selling them for 10$ apiece. These fetched him 800$.

Daymond was astounded at the sales he made and instead of going back home to relax, he instead went back home to sow some more clothes and was back to the street the very next hour after he made his first 800$.

It was evident that he had stumbled on gold as business was booming but Daymond wasn't satisfied with his street sales. So, he thought up an idea that would get his clothing line even more exposure. Daymond started hitting the sets of music videos during the day to persuade the musicians to wear his shirts in their videos so that their fans could see them. This idea was a genius one as his clothes were worn by the biggest and most influential personalities who had a direct impact on their target audience. Needless to say, his success skyrocketed after that.

In spite of his company's success, Daymond still waited tables at Red Lobster serving customers food items that ranged from shrimps to biscuits as well as anything else they needed. He just didn't think he should quit his job at the very beginning even though he was already making a head way with the business but he eventually did when the business demanded more of his attention and effort.

Daymond's hustle helped him turn a small operation based out of his mom's home into a booming business, bringing in $350 million in revenue within six years. Today, FUBU has earned over $6 billion in global sales.

FUBU brand popularity

While his brand's popularity faded out in the early 2000s, Daymond as a person did not as he reinvented himself and has today become the face of American entrepreneurship.

He has several portfolios under his belt including a multi-million dollar empire that encompasses fashion and media amongst other things. He is also renowned for his role as an "investor" (shark) on one of the biggest and most widely acclaimed reality show to ever come out of America. Recently also, President Obama named him "Global Ambassador of Entrepreneurship" -- a move John says he never could have imagined when he was growing up.

All these he achieved as a result of his penchant for hard work. Noteworthy is the fact that he struggled with dyslexia in his early years. A condition that made him struggled to read and write but in spite of this, he still climbed to the pinnacle of success.

Why do I tell you all these now? It is so that you can see that there really isn't anything that can stop you from attaining fulfillment & success in life if you can put in the work. With sheer determination to work hard, you can be sure to succeed at whatever you set your mind upon in no time.

"The price of success is hard work, dedication to the job at hand and the determination that whether we win or lose, we have applied the best of ourselves to the task at hand."

– Vincent Lombardi.

A hard working man is a rich man because he can through hard work discover himself and the hidden potentials within him. Moreover, hard work is the gift that God gave to humanity because through it we discover the hidden resources in the earth and we can then begin to unearth them.

Think about it for a moment, all the natural resources and precious stones in the world are never found on the surface of the earth. It is only those who have invested the time and resources to go deep into the soil that ever find them. It is those who have put in the work that ever get to reach these precious stones.

Even after these resources have been found, it takes hard work to refine these hidden resources into objects of beauty. Until hard work is put in, we can't enjoy the benefits and beauties of these precious stones even though we have them in our hands.

Also through hard work, we are able to make the world a better place as we produce products for other people and we are able to feed ourselves and our families. Needless to say, hard work is an essential ingredient in self-fulfillment. It doesn't matter what gifts you possess, if you cannot work hard, you will never come to fulfillment.

Conclusion:
A Different Side To
Self-fulfillment

Conclusion: A Different Side To Self-fulfillment

By now, you can boldly say that you have been equipped and armed with the tips to a successful and fulfilling life. As a matter of fact, you can be rest assured that the application of the principles shared in this book will guarantee you of an upward and forward life only.

"The will to win, the desire to succeed, the urge to reach your full potential… these are the keys that will unlock the door to personal excellence."

– Confucius

I will like to further express however, that though I have endeavored to show you the way, you have to walk the walk. You have to put what you have learnt to work. Not just for a moment or while the knowledge is still fresh but for a long time. You will need to make these a set of principles that govern your entire life. And the guarantee that I gave you is that you will never regret it or look back.

"I firmly believe that any man's finest hour, the greatest fulfillment of all that he holds dear, is that moment when he has worked his heart out in a good cause and lies exhausted on the field of battle – victorious."

-Vince Lombardi

Thank you for reading this far. I really can't wait to hear what becomes of you through the application of these laws and secrets. Feel free to write me at any time to my personal email – **pastor@godembassy.org**

You can also avail yourself of other training materials of mine available on my blog at **SundayAdelajaBlog.com**

SUNDAY ADELAJA'S
BIOGRAPHY

Pastor Sunday Adelaja is the Founder and Senior Pastor of The Embassy of the Blessed Kingdom of God for All Nations Church in Kyiv, Ukraine.

Sunday Adelaja is a Nigerian-born Leader, Thinker, Philosopher, Transformation Strategist, Pastor, Author and Innovator who lives in Kiev, Ukraine.

At 19, he won a scholarship to study in the former Soviet Union. He completed his master's program in Belorussia State University with distinction in journalism.

At 33, he had built the largest evangelical church in Europe — The Embassy of the Blessed Kingdom of God for All Nations.

Sunday Adelaja is one of the few individuals in our world who has been privileged to speak in the United Nations, Israeli Parliament, Japanese Parliament and the United States Senate.

The movement he pioneered has been instrumental in reshaping lives of people in the Ukraine, Russia and about 50 other nations where he has his branches.

His congregation, which consists of ninety-nine percent white Europeans, is a cross-cultural model of the church for the 21st century.

His life mission is to advance the Kingdom of God on earth by raising a generation of history makers who will live for a cause larger, bigger and greater than themselves. Those who will live like Jesus and transform every sphere of the society in every nation as a model of the Kingdom of God on earth.

His economic empowerment program has succeeded in raising over 200 millionaires in the short period of three years.

Sunday Adelaja is the author of over 300 books, many of which are translated into several languages including Russian, English, French, Chinese, German, etc.

His work has been widely reported by world media outlets such as The Washington Post, The Wall Street Journal, New York Times, Forbes, Associated Press, Reuters, CNN, BBC, German, Dutch and French national television stations.

Pastor Sunday is happily married to his "Princess" Bose Dere-Adelaja. They are blessed with three children: Perez, Zoe and Pearl.

Bill Clinton — 42Nd President Of The United States (1993–2001), Former Arcansas State Governor

Ariel "Arik" Sharon — Israeli Politician, Israeli Prime Minister (2001–2006)

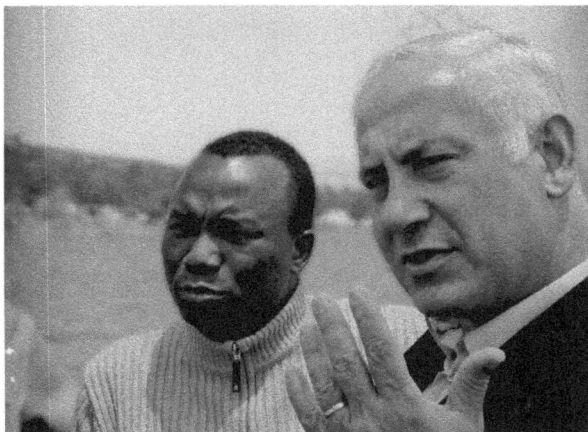

Benjamin Netanyahu — Statesman Of Israel. Israeli Prime Minister (1996–1999), Acting Prime Minister (From 2009)

Jean ChrEtien —
Canadian Politician,
20Th Prime Minister Of
Canada, Minister Of Justice
Of Canada, Head Of Liberan
Party Of Canada

Rudolph Giuliani —
American Political Actor,
Mayor Of New York Served
From 1994 To 2001. Actor
Of Republican Party

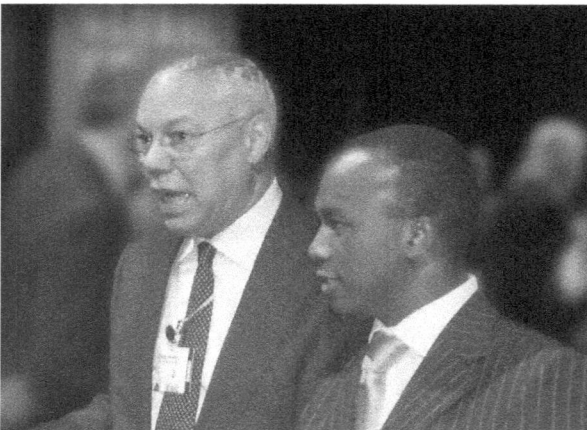

Colin Powell —
Is An American Statesman
And A Retired Four-Star
General In The Us Army,
65Th United States Secretary
Of State

Peter J. Daniels —
Is A Well-Known And
Respected Australian
Christian International
Business Statesman Of
Substance

Madeleine
Korbel Albright —
An American Politician And
Diplomat, 64Th United States
Secretary Of State

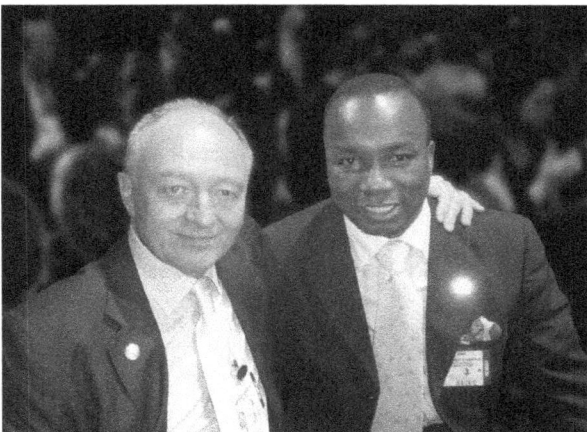

Kenneth Robert
Livingstone —
An English Politician,
1St Mayor Of London
(4 May 2000 – 4 May
2008), Labour Party
Representative

Sir Richard Charles Nicholas Branson —
English Business Magnate, Investor And Philanthropist. He Founded The *Virgin Group,* Which Controls More Than 400 Companies

Mel Gibson —
American Actor And Filmmaker

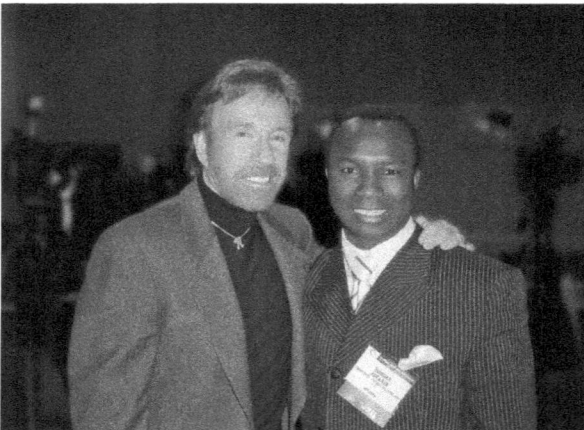

Chuck Norris —
American Martial Artist, Actor, Film Producer And Screenwriter

Christopher Tucker — American Actor And Comedian

Bernice Albertine King — American Minister Best Known As The Youngest Child Of Civil Rights Leaders Martin Luther King Jr. And Coretta Scott King Andrew

Andrew Young — American Politician, Diplomat, And Activist, 14[Th] United States Ambassador To The United Nations, 55[Th] Mayor Of Atlanta

General Wesley Kanne Clark — 4-Star General And Nato Supreme Allied Commander

Dr. Sunday Adelaja's family: Perez, Pearl, Zoe and Pastor Bose Adelaja

FOLLOW
SUNDAY ADELAJA
ON SOCIAL MEDIA

Subscribe And Read Pastor Sunday's Blog:
www.sundayadelajablog.com

**Follow these links and listen to over 200
of Pastor Sunday`s Messages free of charge:**
http://sundayadelajablog.com/content/

Follow Pastor Sunday on Twitter:
www.twitter.com/official_pastor

**Join Pastor Sunday's Facebook
page to stay in touch:**
www.facebook.com/
pastor.sunday.adelaja

**Visit our websites for more
information about Pastor
Sunday's ministry:**
http://www.godembassy.com
http://www.
pastorsunday.com
http://sundayadelaja.de

CONTACT

FOR DISTRIBUTION OR TO ORDER
BULK COPIES OF THIS BOOK,
PLEASE CONTACT US:

USA
CORNERSTONE PUBLISHING
info@thecornerstonepublishers.com
+1 (516) 547-4999
www.thecornerstonepublishers.com

AFRICA
SUNDAY ADELAJA MEDIA LTD.
E-mail: btawolana@hotmail.com
+2348187518530, +2348097721451, +2348034093699

LONDON, UK
PASTOR ABRAHAM GREAT
abrahamagreat@gmail.com
+447711399828, +441908538141

KIEV, UKRAINE
pa@godembassy.org
Mobile: +380674401958

BEST SELLING BOOKS BY DR. SUNDAY ADELAJA
AVAILABLE ON AMAZON.COM AND OKADABOOKS.COM

Best Selling Books by Dr. Sunday Adelaja
Available on Amazon.com and Okadabooks.com

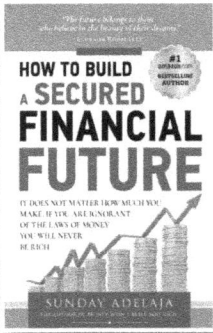

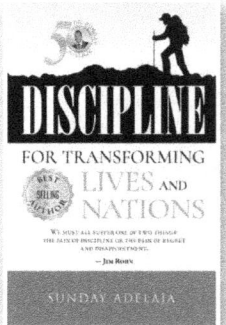

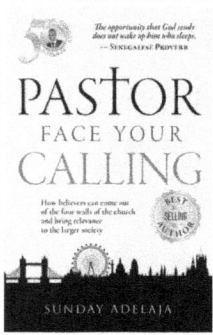

HOW TO BUILD A SECURED FINANCIAL FUTURE
IT DOES NOT MATTER HOW MUCH YOU MAKE IF YOU ARE IGNORANT OF THE LAWS OF MONEY YOU WILL NEVER BE RICH
SUNDAY ADELAJA

CREATE YOUR OWN NET WORTH
YOUR MONEY IS TEMPORARY, YOUR NET WORTH IS ETERNAL
SUNDAY ADELAJA

RAISING THE NEXT GENERATION OF STEVE JOBS AND BILL GATES
HOW TO CONVERT YOUR INNER ENERGY INTO TANGIBLE PRODUCTS
SUNDAY ADELAJA

POVERTY MINDSET vs ABUNDANCE MINDSET
REAL POVERTY IS NOT IN THE SIZE OF YOUR POCKET BUT IN THE SIZE OF YOUR MIND
SUNDAY ADELAJA

WHY YOU MUST URGENTLY BECOME A WORKAHOLIC
SUNDAY ADELAJA

HOW TO BECOME GREAT THROUGH TIME CONVERSION
Are you WASTING TIME, SPENDING TIME OR INVESTING TIME?
SUNDAY ADELAJA

The NIGERIAN ECONOMY THE WAY FORWARD
TAKING NIGERIA FROM ECONOMIC RECESSION INTO GLOBAL ECONOMIC DOMINANCE
SUNDAY ADELAJA

DISCIPLINE FOR TRANSFORMING LIVES AND NATIONS
SUNDAY ADELAJA

PASTOR FACE YOUR CALLING
How believers can come out of the four walls of the church and bring relevance to the larger society
SUNDAY ADELAJA

FOR DISTRIBUTION OR TO ORDER BULK COPIES OF THIS BOOKS, PLEASE CONTACT US:

USA | CORNERSTONE PUBLISHING
E-mail: info@thecornerstonepublishers.com, +1 (516) 547-4999
www.thecornerstonepublishers.com

AFRICA | SUNDAY ADELAJA MEDIA LTD.
E-mail: btawolana@hotmail.com
+2348187518530, +2348097721451, +2348034093699

LONDON, UK | PASTOR ABRAHAM GREAT
E-mail: abrahamagreat@gmail.com, +447711399828, +441908538141

KIEV, UKRAINE |
E-mail: pa@godembassy.org, Mobile: +380674401958

GOLDEN JUBILEE SERIES BOOKS
BY DR. SUNDAY ADELAJA

FOR DISTRIBUTION OR TO ORDER BULK COPIES OF THIS BOOKS, PLEASE CONTACT US:

USA | CORNERSTONE PUBLISHING
E-mail: info@thecornerstonepublishers.com, +1 (516) 547-4999
www.thecornerstonepublishers.com

AFRICA | SUNDAY ADELAJA MEDIA LTD.
E-mail: btawolana@hotmail.com
+2348187518530, +2348097721451, +2348034093699

LONDON, UK | PASTOR ABRAHAM GREAT
E-mail: abrahamagreat@gmail.com, +447711399828, +441908538141

KIEV, UKRAINE |
E-mail: pa@godembassy.org, Mobile: +380674401958

www.ingramcontent.com/pod-product-compliance
Lightning Source LLC
Chambersburg PA
CBHW022112608042 6
4273 4CB000006B/245